Bars in the Sun

By Phil Rogers

Contact: philrogers1622@gmail.com

Published 19th January 2016

Table of Contents

The Dream Is Over

Planning the Dream

It's Moving Along

We're Off

Solicitors and Shopping

Boxto

The Summer is Coming

July - The Spanish are coming

Taking Off Now

Winter Approaches

The New Year

The Sale

Boxto the Final Story

Final Thoughts

The Dream Is Over

It's almost over. One and a half years of 'Living the Dream' in Spain running a restaurant and bar in Fuengirola. I'm starting near the end of my adventure as the next few paragraphs provide a great summary of the reality of this dream.

It's July 2006 and I'm sat by the side of the road in a desolate lay-by halfway between the coast road and Ronda on the Costa del Sol waiting for the wagon to transport my car back to the U.K. My mate for the last 2 years Jim pulls up next to my car to give me a lift back to Fuengirola. The wagon is due at 1pm and I wait with anticipation for it to hopefully arrive on time. At 1300 hrs on the dot the transporter appears as a tiny dot driving up the main road and I wave frantically at the driver who smiles and returns my greeting. I quickly return to my car to remove some personal belongings only to look back in horror as the transporter continues past me driving up the road until out of sight heading for Ronda.

Jim shouts over to me. 'Phil was that him? Where the hell is he off to?'

I reply 'God knows I am sure he saw me'.

Picking up my phone I frantically ring my contact number over and over but there is just voicemail.

We wait beside the road in 80 degree heat hoping that the transporter returns. We wait for 1 hour, then 2 becoming more and more desperate.

'Got to get back by 5', Jim pipes up.

'Give it another half hour', I plead. 'I'll pay for your beer all night'.

'OK another 30 minutes then I'm off', he says quietly.

My phone rings. It's the driver saying he's 5 minutes away and at the top of the hill the transporter appears heading our way.

We both rush to the side of the road ready to jump out in front of the wagon to make sure it stops as the driver slowly pulls into the lay by. The transporter is loaded with five other expensive looking vehicles, three Mercedes, one Audi and one BMW 5 series. My four year old Peugeot 206 did not seem to be worth the cost of transporting it back to the UK when compared to this lot.

The driver's mate jumps down from the wagon and moves back towards the main road looking up and down as the driver slowly steps down from his cab and begins to carefully check over his vehicle to make sure everything is secure.

I look on in surprise as the driver shouts over.

'Worse than the bloody scousers these bastards'.

His mate shouted back, 'Looks good to go', and the driver releases the locking mechanism at the back of the transporter ready to load my car up beside the other five.

'Got an iron bar in the cab, ready for these thieving gets. They bloody love these 'mercs''.

'The Spanish', I reply. My response is based on a very educated guess based on my last two years living in Spain.

'Yes', the driver replies, 'Like I say, you think the scousers are bad. They are like angels compared to these buggers'.

This conversation to me two years ago would have been a bit of a surprise, but I understood without any further discussion just what he meant after trying to run a business in Spain.

The driver quickly loaded my car onto the wagon, while his mate continued to scan up and down the road looking for any Spanish scallies.

'All done, let's go', the driver calls to his mate as they both jump back into the cab.

'Good luck', he shouts over to me and Jim as he pulls onto the main road and heads back down to the coast.

I jump into the car beside Jim as we follow him back down to the coast road and head back to Fuengirola.

Now if I had had that conversation 2 years ago I would probably have reconsidered my decision to move to Spain. However it's all done now and I am alive to tell the tale to other dreamers who think that doing what I did is 'Living the Dream' or maybe it's really something else.

I'll let you decide over the next few chapters.

Planning the Dream

It was probably a late mid life crisis at 50 but I had convinced myself that running a bar or restaurant in Spain would be both exciting and relaxing. After 30 years in IT and a heart attack to boot my dream was to live and work in the sun, by the sea and see out my days away from the rainy UK and planned to try this for the next 10 years before I was ready to retire.

My great idea was to buy a restaurant and bar, one for me and the wife, Barbara, and one for my eldest son, Steve who at 24 years old also seemed to be having an early mid life crisis working in a mobile phone call centre.

So armed with nothing more than visits to a few web sites which incidentally had hundreds of businesses for sale I set forth with my wife and sister also called Barbara to explore these fantastic opportunities on the Costa del Sol. I spoke at length to Robbie, a cockney character who was the director of an operation called 'Bars in the Sun' based in Fuengirola to arrange a meeting at his office.

It was February 2005 when we drove up to Manchester and battling through snow and hail we managed to reach the airport ready to fly away from the dreary UK.

Soon we were on our way to Malaga where we picked up our rental car ready to meet up with Robbie from 'Bars in the Sun' later that day and David from 'Spanish Bars', a second operator, the following day in sunny Fuengirola.

We stored our winter clothes in the car and headed into the sun along the coast ready for our first adventure.

The mobile rang. It was Robbie.

'Where are you?' he said, 'Lots to see today', and we arranged to meet by McDonalds at 2pm. We parked up and waited for Robbie to arrive. After 30 minutes a figure appeared up the road shouting and waving frantically. It was Robbie. We had been waiting for him at the wrong McDonald's. Great start.

'Nice to meet you, Phil, welcome to paradise', chirped Robbie. 'Let's get on with it, lots to see'.

We shook hands and followed him to his car to begin our viewings of four or five of these fantastic opportunities.

We hit a local bar first up a narrow side street off the main drag where we met a sullen Spanish chap sat reading his paper outside his premises.

Inside was a bar stocked with only a few random bottles of spirits, a few stools and obviously no customers.

'If you put some food on here this place would be a bloody goldmine', said Robbie in an upbeat manner.

Robbie chatted to the proprietor who laughed and nodded. 'Si, si', he spouted.

'Got any books, accounts, to look at?' I asked.

Robbie and the owner of the bar laughed.

'This is Spain....books, accounts..what are those?'

'I make 500 euros a night and double in the summer', said the chap in Spanish which Robbie translated back to me.

'Bollocks', I thought to myself and suggested we move on.

Next we moved on to a bar on the promenade on the sea front.

It was a large sort of cocktail bar, called Lacy's. Inside there was a 'pole' stuck in the middle of a small stage and lots of scruffy, stained, pseudo satin chairs and sofas.

The owner Jose led us away from this area down some stairs towards the basement. The basement was made up of four or five what looked like prison cells each with a small bed and broken table.

'This is the entertainment area', chuckled Jose in broken English. 'This is where we make the money'.

Robbie winked at me knowingly as my sister who had no idea about the purpose of this place said her idea would be to fill the area with pool tables and slot machines.

No one replied.

We wandered back up the steps as there was an offer to look at the books.

Jose produced his laptop with a clear set of day to day accounts.

Monday's takings 40 euros
Tuesday's takings 65 euros
Saturday's takings 75 euros

I looked on in astonishment wondering why someone who was selling this place to me would produce such a rubbish set of accounts.

Robbie could see my puzzled face and piped up.

'Don't worry....the main accounts for down stairs are a secret', repeating his standard phrase. 'This place is a little gold mine'.

We left the bar and went off for a quick snack after arranging to meet up with Robbie again in one hour for more viewings.

My wife, sister and I ordered a quick sandwich and coffee and sat down to reflect on the day so far.

'I liked Lacy's', piped up my sister. 'Just needs a few changes downstairs'.

'It's a brothel', I said quietly as slowly her expression changed as the realisation of what we had actually been looking at dawned on her.

'The pole gives it away a bit, don't you think'.

'My god', she said. 'It didn't cross my mind'.

Soon we were off with Robbie further down the coast to Los Boliches to look at another restaurant, Las Maniera. This looked a bit more promising as we pulled up outside a restaurant overlooking the sea.

We wandered through into the main area which actually smelled a bit like rotten fish towards the bar which was decorated in a South sea Island style with cane decor which itself seemed to be a bit mouldy and broken in some places behind the bar.

An old man Pedro greeted us smiling and in broken English started his obviously pre prepared monologue.

'Very cheap...very good...lots of dinero (money) for you', spouted Pedro over and over as we looked around his restaurant. It was obvious that there had not been much investment in the place, particularly cleaning services. We wandered downstairs into a basement which hosted a pool table which had seen better days and two dust covered tables with empty bottles which looked as if they had resided there for some time.

At the back of the property we stumbled upon the highlight of the tour. There were two enclosed private parking bays. Hurrah…

The tour lasted about ten minutes and Robbie could see the disappointment increasing as our conversations became less upbeat.

He jumped onto his phone and made a couple of desperate phone calls back to base.

'Right', he said. 'We have got a quick viewing arranged now back in Fuengirola but there is an offer on the place so we have to be quick and I can't make any promises'.

We dashed back to the car and sped back along the coast. We parked on the front and wandered behind the Hotel Del Puerto where there was a street full of restaurants.

'This is 'Fish Alley' have you heard of it, 'Hungry Street, Calle Moncayo'. It was about 5 o'clock now and our hopes were raised as we looked down along a street rammed full of restaurants. Chinese, Spanish, Indian, Swedish etc etc. More importantly there were for the first time quite a few tourists wandering up and down looking at the different menus on offer.

We wandered past a few restaurants until we came to the 'Dom Miguel'. The place was designed mainly in wood, and looked like a combination of a Spanish tapas bar and a Swiss chalet. There was a long bar with about 30 tables set up ready for business, seating fifty inside and twenty five on the terrace. Lots of wooden wine racks populated the walls with a sparse range of wines and there was similar racking behind the bar.

We met George the owner who looked the spitting image of Bobby George the darts player. He was dripping in gold and could just about communicate in broken English.

Behind the bar was a Chinese guy called Hue and just arriving the Moroccan chef, Hamed.

George made the introductions and explained the history of the place which had been completely refurbished 18 months ago. He took us all into the kitchen which looked brand new with Hamed smiling and uttering 'Very good. Good work. Good kitchen', while he peeled some carrots ready for the evening trade.

'Any books to look at?' I asked George who in the usual Spanish style smiled back at me obviously thinking that this was a stupid question.

'No books', he said. 'This is Spain'.

'Well what are the takings?' I replied.

'1,000 euros a night easy, and we do not open one day a week. Double in the summer', said George. 'If you decided to open during the day as well you could make much more', he added.

George explained that there had been an offer and they were waiting for the 10% deposit from the potential buyer which was due to arrive within two days. As far as he was concerned the restaurant was still for sale until he had this cash in his pocket.

This all looked better and Robbie could see our mood changing.

'OK, that's it for today, have a think tonight and call me 1st thing tomorrow'.

Feeling tired now we realised we had not had time to book anywhere to stay the night and Robbie ushered us back to the car and drove us to a good 'hostel' mid way between Fuengirola and Los Boliches. He dropped us off and we booked in for the night.

Hostels in Spain are just cheap mini hotels normally with a small bar in the front reception area, and generally half decent accommodation.

It was dark now around 7pm as we all quickly showered and changed ready for the night of discovery ahead.

It was almost 8pm and quite cold as we planned our itinerary for the night. We decided to pay a visit to Las Marinas which was only 200 metres from the hostel. We walked quickly along the coast and found a bar just across from the restaurant where we sat and staked out the joint.

It was empty with just Pedro and another guy sat at a table chatting and drinking. We sat for 30 minutes finishing our drinks and counted around 10 people wandering past the restaurant, some stopping at adjoining eateries. No one entered the Las Marinas. It was completely deserted.

'Remember it's February', piped up wife Barbara.

'Then why bother opening', I replied. 'Let's go, we've seen enough'.

We headed back up the coast back towards Fish Alley which was about a half mile away.

We soon reached the start of Fish Alley and we were pleasantly surprised to see quite a few tourists heading down towards the row of restaurants.

A couple of the restaurants were half full, inside only, as the terraces were not being used at this time of the year. One or two of the restaurants were completely empty.

We walked towards the Dom Miguel and sat down at the nearest table inside. The restaurant was quite cosy and had the heating turned on making the place quite comfortable. There were around another five or six tables occupied and the place was reasonably busy considering the time of year.

The menu choice was very varied offering a range of steak, fish, pasta and Spanish dishes and we ordered a mixture of meals between the three of us.

The meals were served promptly and the food was really good, and at a reasonable price. At the end of the meal we were served a free liquor shot which was a nice touch to finish.

Believe it or not, an obvious thought struck me for the first time. 'Bloody chef', I uttered, 'We can't do this ourselves...we need a bloody chef'. Christ what a tosser I thought to myself as I had overlooked this in the excitement of the possible adventure ahead.

'This is it', we all agreed. This is the place to open. Then realisation struck. Robbie said there was an offer on the place. Shit can we do anything.

We couldn't wait. I rang Robbie. It was 10pm.

He answered straight away.

'Hi Phil, what's happened'?

'We want the Dom Miguel. I can send the deposit tomorrow', I shouted desperately.

'Hang on I'll get back to you tomorrow', said Robbie quite reservedly.

'Oh and we want the chef.....we must have the bloody chef', I again shouted.

'Leave it with me..go and get drunk', he laughed...tomorrow'.

The three of us left the Dom Miguel and wandered back down the front back to the hostel.

The next day my phone rang early and to my disappointment it was David, not Robbie who we had also arranged to meet to look for a bar for my son Steve.

'Where are you? I will pick you up..we have four to see, all arranged before 12 this morning', said David knowing that we had the flight arranged for home at 5pm.

We wandered outside into the warm spring like day and waited for David who pulled up within minutes.

We jumped in his car and headed for our quick tour.

'Got some great ones lined up', he piped up, 'but I'll leave the best till last. The first one is down at the harbour...best spot in Fuengirola'.

We parked up and wandered towards the harbour, through a huge car park and down a couple of alleys. The car park itself was lined with a few small run down bars. We arrived at the harbour. Now, a harbour in Spain gives the picture of glamorous yachts with a huge promenade lined with bars and restaurants. In Fuengirola the promenade is about 80 metres in length and about 10 metres wide with a random selection of boats rammed into the available space. It's definitely not Puerto Banus that's for sure...more like an old boatyard.

Back from the tiny promenade, crammed together there were about 20 bars and restaurants running along the length of the car park. Ok it is February I admit but there was literally not a soul in sight apart from the owners looking bored.

We wandered up to a small bar, probably the smallest which had room for two tables inside and four outside. The bar itself was tiny and the proprietors were from Swindon called Eva and John.

David introduced us to the couple.

'Been here one year but need to get back to the UK, family issues. This is an absolute bargain at 25,000 euros. We are packed in the summer', said Eva.

The three of us looked at each other as we reluctantly were shown around the whole joint. In fairness it took about 30 seconds.

'Thanks a lot. We will be in touch', I lied.

We left the grotty port area and wandered back to the car. David took us to two other bars next which to be honest looked exactly the same. 6 metre maximum fronts, a small bar with a few stools and a couple of tables outside.

'Ideal for your son', said David.

'He would be bored stiff, no chance', I replied, and my wife nodded in agreement.

'Right let's go, the next one is the one for you', said David. 'We can walk there from here'.

We headed back along the front and up a main side street just by the 'London Bar' which was actually quite busy. We passed four or five clubs and karaoke bars and just set back from the road came across 'Boxto' pronounced 'Botcho', where three dodgy looking individuals were standing outside who looked as if they had not slept for a week.

We were introduced to Diego, Rodrigo and Rolando the joint lease owners and walked into Boxto. There were no windows and it was quite dark inside.

Inside 'Boxto' was a long bar with stools, quite a large wooden standing/dance area about 25 metres by 15 metres with a raised platform in the corner for the DJ to do his stuff and two toilets and a storeroom on the far wall.

'Fully air conditioned and 8 euros a drink. Let me show you something', said Diego.

Diego, an Italian guy with a greasy ponytail and silly shorts produced an official looking paper.

'160,000 euros turnover and that is just the summer and weekends only in the winter. We have this 12,000 euro tax bill for you to pay in July. 8 euros we charge for every mixed drink. You can't go wrong here,' he spouted.

David explained, '2am to 4am, that is when you make your money. All the other bars have to close at 2. Your license runs until 4am'.

We inspected the official looking document convinced it was genuine.

Diego one of the chaps started some music from the DJ area which was incredibly loud.

'Soundproof ...Boxto...noise no problem'.

We listened to the sales pitch and decided that this was the place for Steve.

'We need to get our son Steve over next week to have a look'.

'Don't worry', said Diego 'We will look after him and help him for a couple of weeks'.

We all shook hands again and spoke to David.

'Looks like you did save the best till last. We'll get Steve across next week to see what he thinks', I said.

We all shook hands and the three of us headed back to our hire car to drive back to Malaga airport and fly back to dreary Britain. First we ring Steve to tell him the news and ask him to have a quick scan on the web for Boxto.

We were all excited by the visit thinking that we could possibly have two places lined up, ready to start our dream. However, Robbie had still not been in touch about the Dom Miguel.

It's Moving Along

It's Tuesday and we all arrive back in the U.K. on time and drive back home, where Steve is waiting by the door in anticipation. He had seen the pictures of Boxto on the net and in his usual exuberant manner was ready to pack and get started straight away.

We sit him down and try to explain that running a bar is not just about loud music and lots of fun but he is well prepared for us to knock back any concerns. His track record managing money is one to behold however.

Look he says excitedly 'Don't worry about a thing, I've got it all sorted', said Steve in his usual upbeat manner.

'My mate, Liam will run the business, stock, ordering, staff and legal stuff. I will be head of marketing to get people in and I will run the bar and make lots of money'.

'Cleaning?' I replied, 'Who has volunteered to do that?'

'Cleaning, we'll both do that', said Steve.

Now Steve's idea of cleaning does not extend beyond remembering to flush the toilet, but we figured that we could pay for a cleaner. Remember 160,000 Euros last year ..no problem.

Liam is a local lad who works in an IT shop. He weighs in at about 16 stone with shocking ginger hair. However, we know him well and he's a nice lad, although I don't think he's travelled much farther than Crewe, two miles away.

'Right', I said, 'Before we do anything lets book to travel back to Spain this weekend with Liam to have a look at the place, particularly between 2 and 4 am when it is supposed to be busy according to them.

The next day at 7am I check my email and there is one from Bars in the Sun. It must be Robby.

'Been trying to ring you', it starts. 'The deposit has not come through from the other chap. Transfer 10% (11,000 euros) and it's yours. Be QUICK!!!!....bank details for you below'.

NB. The chef comes with the restaurant. I guess you still want him.

'Shit'. I run upstairs to tell the two Barbaras.

Let's do it we all agree and my sister asks if we can buy the restaurant 50/50. It's a deal. I'll shoot down to the bank as soon as possible.

I arrive at the bank at 9am. It doesn't open until 9.30.

I wait impatiently as the shutters are raised and head to the counter to arrange the transfer.

'Money should be through by the end of today', the teller confirms.

I race back home and email Robby to tell him the good news.

The rest of the day is spent online booking flights for the Saturday ahead. This time we include Liam and Steve as well as Barbara (wife), Barbara (sister) and Richie her husband who would travel down to my house in Cheshire on the Friday from the north east.

I spend the next few days much more seriously trying to learn Spanish as this time it looks like it is all for real now and arranging meetings for the Saturday with Robbie and David to talk about what happens next and finally booking 3 rooms at the Fuengirola hostel.

Saturday arrives and in two cars we head for the early flight at Manchester airport. The kids, Steve and Liam are buzzing with excitement. We arrive in Malaga and this time take the local train along the coast to Fuengirola.

On booking into the hostel we strolled up to the nightclub, Boxto. It is deserted and the shutters are down as it doesn't open until 10pm. We meet up with Robbie to discuss the Dom Miguel who takes us through the next stages, the key to which was to find a trustworthy, English speaking abogado (solicitor).

Robbie provided a list of services that the abogado should be able to provide including, managing contracts/exchange, submitting accounts, arranging an NIE (Tax registration numbers, and managing transfer of electric, phone and water services into my name.)

Next he tells us to set up two bank accounts one personal and one for the business.

Robbie also took us through the process of paying off the outstanding money owed on the Dom Miguel for the lease which works like this.

The price of the Dom Miguel to me was 110,000 Euros for the thirty year lease.
The price of the Dom Miguel as far as the tax authorities are concerned is 60,000 Euros.
The price paid for the Dom Miguel as far as the chap who owns the freehold is concerned is also 60,000 Euros. He pockets 20% for any sale of the lease i.e. 12,000 Euros.

We also had to take into account the 2,000 euros per month ground rent to be paid to the freeholder and the yearly terrace tax of around 800 euros.

All transactions are done in cash and Robbie finished his master class with 'Don't worry your abogado (solicitor) will manage all of this. If there is a problem we can use my abogado. Also George, the owner of the Dom Miguel has spoken to the freeholder. He is fine with this price'.

I imagine he is, 12,000 Euros for doing bugger all. No wonder Spain and Greece are going bust. I will provide further details of how this 'tax' system operates later in the book.

Organising the legal side was not too difficult as I had previous experience of dealing with an abogado, called Henrique from an outfit called Arriva Abogadas when unsuccessfully looking to buy an apartment a couple of years before in Porte de la Duquesa. He seemed a nice enough chap though a little expensive.

We agreed that the provisional exchange date would be three weeks away on Wednesday 3rd April and we should be ready to go.

I immediately found an internet cafe and drafted an email to Henrique asking for the costs for his services, while Robbie rang the bank to arrange an appointment for me to sort out my new accounts for the next day.

We all drifted back to the hostel to wash and change ready for the night ahead feeling a bit nervous about going back to the Dom Miguel for our evening meal.

We wandered into the cosy restaurant and waited for the waitress to pull together two tables to seat the six of us. George was not around this time but the Chinese guy Hue acknowledged us and the chef Hamed waved from the kitchen.

This time being obviously qualified restaurateurs we critiqued the menu, removing things and making a thousand suggestions for changes including many price increases. The women redesigned the rest of the place ranging from new salt cellars to tablecloths while we all watched the service staff closely to make sure that they knew what they were supposed to be doing.

The core to the menu was a very good selection of starters, mains and deserts which made up the 'menu del dia', (menu of the day), which could be had for a bargain at 7.75 euros including free liquor shots at the end of the meal. This was backed up by an extensive a la carte menu including 3 sexy sounding specials coming in at 23 Euros a shot together with Spanish speciality starters such as Prawn Pil Pil, Mussels and chorizo and of course paella.

The place began filling up slowly, to about a quarter full and we drank and dined feeling happy that the decision we had made was the right one. Remember this was the end of February, we were confident that peak season would be manic.

We finished off the meals, leaving an unusually big tip of course and decided to wander across to Boxto which was just opening ready for the 10pm start.

The three amigos, Diego, Rodrigo and Rolando who we had met previously, were stood behind the bar all appearing to be very busy ready for the Saturday night ahead although the place was empty.

I introduced Steve and Liam to the three guys with Diego who could speak the best English, laughing and joking telling them how great the place was (best bar in Fuengirola) and how much they would be willing to help settle them in for a couple of weeks and show them the ropes. The kids lapped it up.

Now, I would have maybe, just maybe expected a free drink, but no, 50 bloody euros for six drinks. Not much less than the meal (and drinks) we had just had in the Dom Miguel.

Anyway just think of the profits to come. I had seen the accounts remember. Richie, my brother in law, laughingly suggested that they should have gone fifty fifty on Boxto and not the Dom Miguel.

We left the kids chatting to Diego making sure that they were going to return to Boxto between 2am and 4am to get a feel for the 'busy' time and the four of us wandered off for a quick pub crawl around the delights of Fuengirola before returning to the hostel.

The next morning the four of us met up in reception at the hostel for a quick coffee before breakfast waiting for news of the lads' adventures last night.

After half an hour Steve appeared looking bedraggled after his heavy night and was uncharacteristically quiet.

'Well, how was it?' I asked as we all waited in anticipation.

'Really great', Steve responded, 'The place was quite busy. We left at three. Full of mainly Spanish and five or six Brits'.

'Do you want it then?' my wife said.

'Yes, brilliant, it would be perfect, can't wait', replied Steve.

'Where's Liam?' I asked, just as he appeared down the steps, looking quite sheepish.

'What happened to you, you look rough?' I continued.

'Got mugged but only lost a few euros, but I didn't have my card with me thank god', said Liam trying to appear casual.

'God, you Ok', said my wife Barbara.

'Yes no problem just gave them my cash and ran for it. Just unlucky'.

Now, Liam with his ginger hair couldn't be mistaken for anything else but a tourist and be seen as easy pickings by the local louts.

'Where were you, Steve?' said Barbara knowing Steven had a reputation for just wandering off on his own when out drinking with his mates.

'Yes, I was looking for Liam', he said, 'We lost each other for a bit'.

We all looked at each other and agreed that they needed to have a serious chat this morning before we decided to take this any further. Great start.

I then walked with the two Barbaras a mile or so along the coast towards Los Boliches to the Banco Sabadell to open the bank personal and business accounts which was a surprisingly painless process as just the passport was needed for this.

We all flew back to the UK on the Monday buzzing with the prospect of our new lives to come.

We're Off

Back in the UK now with lots to sort out. First sell the house we had owned for the last 6 years and downsize to something we could use as a bolthole back in the UK which we would hopefully never need. My other son, David would live there with his mate while we were in Spain.

Natalia, Henrique's assistant had now emailed back with a breakdown of his legal charges for each of the services requested which in total amounted to around 6,500 euros.

Steve and Liam were ready to go ahead despite the mugging and I agreed that we would move forward with the lease purchase for Boxto four weeks after taking on the Dom Miguel. This would give us some time to get up and running in the restaurant.

Off went another email to Henrique requesting more prices. This time to manage the Boxto contract.

I was hit with another surprise from Steve at this point.

'What about my loans for the car and other things?'

'What other things?' I said.

Now Steve had never been very good to say the least at managing money and was a victim of the banking crisis which surfaced a couple of years later who at the time would have loaned money to my pet dog if it were able to speak.

'Well I've got a big consolidated loan, to cover the car and pay off some other loans and I have got three credit cards maxed out', said Steve

'How much?' I said.

'It's about £7,000', he replied quietly.

'Oh god, guess we will have to pay that off', I said. 'You sure that's it, let me see all of your paperwork, statements, everything'.

For the next three weeks I was glued to the laptop learning more and more Spanish, especially food and drink until I felt quite confident that I would be able to at least make myself understood.

My wife Barbara never quite convinced that the whole thing was a good idea went along with the plan to keep me happy.

March ended quickly and as we moved into April the excitement grew.

My sister Barbara travelled down two days before to stay with us ready for the flight to Malaga from Manchester and to help in the restaurant for the next two weeks while we got settled.

The next morning we drove into Crewe to transfer around 60,000 Euros each into our newly opened Banco Sabadell business account in Fuengirola to cover the lease purchase, legal and start-up costs for our new venture.

I emailed the bank in Spain four hours later to make sure that the money had arrived in the Spanish account and requested that we wanted to withdraw 100,000 euros in cash in two days time.

By the end of the day I had received confirmation from the bank that the money had arrived in the Spanish account and they would have the cash ready for us the day after next as requested at 10am….all in cash.

We arranged to meet up with Robbie and the abogado, Henrique at his office in Fuengirola on the 3rd at 2pm. Robbie confirmed all was set and George the current leaseholder would be there together with the freeholder for his cut from the deal. Robbie also arranged to meet us at the bank at 10am to ferry us to his office and provide a bit more security while the cash was in transit from the bank to his office.

Robbie also offered to show us some apartments in Fuengirola to rent with immediate effect for a small, undisclosed fee to his company of course for the service. Robbie confirmed that we could arrange the viewings for Tuesday 2nd, the day before the contracts were due to be exchanged.

Only packing to worry about now and I made sure to include my laptop, printer (for menus) and laminator in the hand luggage.

The day of the move arrived, Monday 1st April, April Fools day, as we gave last minute instructions to Steve and David to take care of the house while we were away and gave them an idiots guide as to how the washing machine and iron actually worked. The plan was for my wife Barbara to come back after two weeks to look after the house sale and organise the move to the smaller house and join me in Spain later.

We waved goodbye to the kids and the three of us headed for Manchester airport to fly to Malaga and our new life.

The First Few Days

We arrived at Malaga on time at 2pm and caught the train to Fuengirola loaded with tightly packed suitcases and hand luggage. Firstly we booked into the hostel ready for a relaxing night ahead before beginning our new working life.

It was a rainy evening as we set off to visit our new venture and the streets were quiet. It was now around 8pm and this time we started at the other end of Fish Alley. We decided to eat at one of our competitors restaurants and there was lots of choice along the street, to critique their offerings.

We ended up at the Don Pe restaurant, around 50 metres from the Dom Miguel which was quite busy and sat down to test their 'Menu del Dia' which looked quite similar to what was on the menu in our new restaurant. It was pretty good so we realised that we had some competition here. Eight euros for the 3 course menu with a free bottle of wine thrown in. We started speaking to a couple at the next table who told us that they were regulars at the Don Pe and asked if they had tried the Dom Miguel.

'Ah, that's the one with frozen vegetables isn't it? We tried it just the once...no free wine from what I remember either', said the young lady.

Upon finishing we strolled past the Dom Miguel which had around 4 busy tables with two waiting staff standing by the door ready to greet any new customers.

The next day we met up with Robbie at his office to look at rental accommodation. His wife, Sonia, took the lead stating that she had three viewings lined up for the day. I'm still not convinced that renting properties was a part of their core business or that they were making the most of an opportunity to make a bit of easy cash. However regardless I felt that this was not the time to discuss this, as we had a big day tomorrow and needed accommodation fast.

We walked down to the front with Sonia and came to the first apartment block which overlooked the sea and was within easy walking distance of the Dom Miguel.

The lift took us to the 4th floor to view the first apartment. The apartment was fairly non descript with a lounge/dining area, bathroom and two bedrooms. The highlight was the balcony looking over the sand and sea.

'1400 euros per month, plus electric and water costs. Not bad considering the view from here. 1 month deposit in advance, like the U.K.', said Sonia.

Sonia could see the look of indifference on our faces and suggested we move to the next viewing.

This time no more than thirty metres along the front from the first apartment we entered a door at the side of a 'Salsa Music Bar'. Again we entered the lift which took us up to the 5th floor. The apartment was pretty much identical to the previous viewing.

'900 euros for this one, plus services', said Sonia.

'Why such a difference?' I asked.

'Oh it's just that this landlord is keen to rent this place out, hence the good price. You can move in straight away if you want'.

'Sounds good', I said and the three of us agreed that this was the place we wanted.

Now the real reason it was actually cheaper which we found out on the second day was due to two things not mentioned.

Firstly, the incessant din from the Salsa bar on the ground floor until 2 in the morning and secondly the two flats next door were being refurbished and the noise from tiles being removed with a hammer and chisel went on for most of the day. It was like a Japanese torture which went on and on for weeks. I could never figure out how so many tiles could possibly be in such a small apartment.

A quick call from Sonia and as if by magic within minutes the smiling landlord appeared.

'Anything you need just call me..no problem', said the landlord.

The landlord and Sonia went into a quick huddle.

'Do we have British TV?' I asked.

The landlord quickly walked over to the TV set and after a few minutes managed to find the one and only UK channel, 'The Travel Channel' available.

'There you go', the landlord responded with a satisfied look on his face.

I didn't have time to argue so just thanked him for his efforts.

'That will be 2,700 euros including the deposit and my fees', piped up Sonia. 900 euros for Robbie for two hours work, not bad if you can get it.

'Ok', I said and handed over the money and received a receipt from the landlord.

'It's yours, you can move in now if you want. Here are the keys', said Sonia as we all shook hands.

'See you tomorrow for the big signing', said Sonia as she left the apartment, as we all moved to sit on the small balcony and take in the view.

'Ok, we'll have to cancel the hostel booking for tonight and then get a few groceries', said my wife, Barbara.

We walked back to the hostel and agreed to pay a nominal 20 euros for the extended stay, picked up the luggage and moved into the apartment.

We all felt that things were moving along nicely as we settled into our new home for the rest of the afternoon.

No drinking tonight we all agreed, big day tomorrow.

The next day we met up with Robbie at his Bar in the Sun office and we all travelled to the Banco Sabadell.

Robbie waited in reception as the three of us were ushered into a back room by Christina the bank manager where in front of us on the table was 100,000 euros all in 50 euro notes.

'Count it out', said Christina, 'Make sure it's all there'.

The three of us each separately counted out the cash, until we were satisfied that it was all present and correct.

'Happy with that', I said as I loaded my small bag with the cash.

We picked up Robbie as we left the bank and he took us all back to his office to secure the money in the safe for the few hours until 2pm when the abogado was due to arrive. So far so good.

Robbie again explained the process for the exchange and we all shook hands as we left for some lunch.

'See you at 2, don't forget', said Robbie laughing as we left his office.

After a leisurely lunch it was 1.30pm and we slowly walked back to Robbie's office where George the current Dom Miguel leaseholder was waiting with one of his gophers, called Rafael. Rafael seemed to be the guy who did all of the jobs that George couldn't be bothered to do. It wasn't long before the freeholder, Lionel turned up ready to pick up his 12,000 euros. He was less than five foot tall and spoke no English.

He greeted us with 'Hola mis Amigos' and with my newly acquired Spanish skills to the surprise of everyone I replied, 'Com estas?'...how are you?'

2pm passed and still no sign of Henrique, the solicitor, and as 2.20pm approached we all became concerned. I rang his office and was told that he was on his way.

We all stood expectantly on the walkway above the street waiting and waiting.

At 3pm in the distance I caught a glimpse of who I assumed to be Henrique as it was almost two years since I last saw him.

Slowly ambling down the street alongside all of the tourists appeared Henrique, looking like a Mafia godfather decked in a shiny three piece suit, immaculately groomed with jet black hair complete with sunglasses.

He waved as he approached and climbed the stairs up to Robbie's office. We shook hands as I introduced him to Robbie and Lionel.

'Where have you been?' I enquired.

'No lunch, stopped for a snack', as he looked at his watch probably for the first time that day, and said jokingly, 'Spanish time'.

Henrique took myself my wife and sister into the office and asked Robbie if he could have five minutes with us for a quick chat before the exchange.

Henrique pulled out the quotation for his services and explained step by step the detail behind each one.
He then proceeded 'line by line' to explain the contract that we were about to sign which was written in Spanish. It was now approaching 4pm and Robbie was becoming a little anxious popping round the door to make sure there were no problems.

'You are all happy to go ahead', said Robbie.

We all nodded, 'Let's go', replied Henrique.

Henrique beckoned Robbie to come back into the shop and asked for the money to be handed over. Slowly he counted the cash and in an upbeat manner exclaimed, 'Now we are ready'.

Firstly, he asked Lionel to join us and handed over his 12,000 euros which he counted quickly and immediately left.

We all sat round the table with Robbie and George with Rafael stood lurking near the door. Henrique quickly ran through the document with George and asked for his signature which he duly provided. Finally, myself, the two Barbaras and Ritchie signed the same document which was the final part of the exchange.

Finally Henrique gave George the balance of 87,000 euros in cash, which he handed to Rafael to check.

Henrique rose up from his chair extended his hand and said smiling, 'Good luck with the Dom Miguel. Is there anything else you need?'

We all shook our heads and thanked him for his time as he left the office.

'When do you want to open?' said George.

As soon as possible we all replied.

'OK, meet me in the restaurant at 7 tonight and we will discuss a plan with the chef Hamed, his kitchen assistant Halima and Hue the barman', said George. 'I will also ask if Everaldo our resident waiter can be there as well.'

Robbie and George stayed behind to sort out Robbie's commission as the three of us left the office and headed back to our new apartment.

At 7pm on the dot we walked into the Dom Miguel which was closed for business. George and the rest of the team were chatting by the kitchen and they welcomed us warmly.

George who was of Moroccan origin introduced us to Everaldo the resident Brazilian waiter, Hamed the chef and Halima the kitchen assistant. Everaldo spoke perfect Spanish and English as well as his native Portuguese and Hamed informed us that he spoke many, many languages. Halima spoke only Arabic and basic Spanish.

To be honest we all felt very lucky to have these experienced staff at our disposal and readily agreed to sort out the transfer of working contracts over the next few days. Rafael, the gopher, agreed to help us to manage the transfer of the work permits.

Even though there were our three extra pairs of hands available the other waitress currently employed by George would not be joining us and none of us were confident we were ready to do the job.

As I was standing in the bar I noticed a large hole in the ceiling above the bar and a second smaller hole in the ceiling at the restaurant entrance. George picked up on this issue and spoke briefly to Rafael in Arabic.

'This will be fixed tomorrow, don't worry. Is there anything else you need?' as he picked up his phone and called his maintenance contacts.

'Thanks for that', I said 'What about the existing stock, wine etc. How much do we owe you'?

'Free of charge', said George.

I then turned to Hamed and asked him when we could be ready to open.

'Manana', he replied, 'tomorrow', 'If you do some shopping in the morning. Halima and I can start early at 2pm and do the prep ready to open at 6pm'. Everaldo nodded in agreement and Hue the barman agreed to work with us for a couple of nights to show us the ropes.

'I will pick you up from here at 9am tomorrow and we will hit Macro in Malaga and a few other shops. Bring about 700 euros with you', said Hue.

'Oh by the way I will ring San Miguel now to replenish the beer and soft drinks. You pay cash on delivery', said Hue. 'We'll will pick up the wine tomorrow at Carrefour supermarket. Better make that 800 euros'.

'You will need a car, trust me', he laughed.

'Oh, and I'll ring Pescaro to order the fish, prawns and mussels for delivery tomorrow', said Hamed, 'And before I forget someone needs to be here for 12 am tomorrow to pay for the gas and take delivery of the drinks from San Miguel. I'll put the empty gas bottles at the door ready before I go'.

George added 'Can you be here at 10am tomorrow. My guys will be here to fix the ceiling', looking at the two Barbaras.

They both nodded.

'See you at 9 tomorrow', I said to Hue as Hamed passed me a shopping list written in both Spanish and English, three pages long.

'The two Barbaras will be here before 9 tomorrow as well, while I do the shopping with Hue. Looks like we have a plan.'

'OK', said Hue, 'Let me show you how to open up the place before you go. Here are the keys and alarm settings'. We followed Hue who took us through the series of locks and alarms to open and close the shutters and doors into the restaurant.

'I will be here at 5 tomorrow, ready to work', said Everaldo, the waiter, as I moved towards the door looking nervously at the shopping list.

'Hasta manana' (until tomorrow) they said as one as we left the restaurant.

'Shit', I thought, it's all for real now. I'd better make the best use of Hue before he leaves.

The next morning I woke early and sat on the apartment balcony watching the stragglers heading for home after a hard night's clubbing, many of whom looked as if they had spent the night on the beach.

Sister and wife Barbara appeared a little nervous about whether they had remembered the instructions as to how to open up the Dom Miguel ready for the deliveries.

I handed them 200 euros to pay the suppliers and headed off to meet Hue looking forward to my days shopping, which although I didn't realise at this point would take over half of my life for the next two years.

Hue was waiting as promised beside the garage where he kept his Berlingo van.

'Here, you can keep this for now, but you will need to get your own', said Hue as he handed me his Macro card and we sped off along the coast road towards Malaga.

The journey took about 20 minutes and I made a note of the directions for future trips.

We entered Macro with two empty shopping trolleys. The place was massive with around forty aisles packed high with everything you could imagine. I handed him the list and we headed towards the fresh meat section.

'Solomillo,(fillet steak) ternera,(sirloin steak) cerdo,(pork) chuletas de cerdo,(pork chops) chuletas de cordero,(lamb chops) tocino,(bacon) jamón(ham) as he whizzed up and down the aisles loading the trolley with great slabs of a variety of meats. The trolley was already half full. Again, I was struggling to follow him while trying to mark down the aisle numbers against each item as best as I could.

We had only just started…..30 tins of button mushrooms, 50 cartons of tomato puree, 20 cartons of cream, anchovies, cooking oil (20 litres), olive oil, lasagne, rice, vinegar, flour, eggs, mayonnaise, cheese, pate, butter both slabs and individual portions, paper tablecloths, toothpicks, vodka, gin, bacardi etc etc. Lots of different spices I had never heard of and on and on it went until we had almost filled the second trolley.

My writing became less and less distinct and I began to worry about what I had taken on.

I said to Hue 'Thank god that's over, have you been doing this yourself for the past few months'.

Hue smiled and replied, 'Come on we haven't started yet'.

We hit the checkout, handed over 500 euros and dumped everything in the back of the Berlingo.

We sped off towards Malaga town heading for Carrefour which was the wine stop.

24 bottles red, 24 bottles white, 12 bottles rose house wines plus an assortment of more expensive other bottles were loaded into the van.

'Right, back to Fuengirola', said Hue as we set off back down the coast road.

My sense of direction was now completely mixed up as I struggled to remember the routes we had just taken.

'We are nearly done, Lidl next, it's cheaper', said Hue calmly.

We headed for the Lidl store which sits just outside of Fuengirola.

'2 trolleys', shouted Hue as we rushed into the store.

'Right', said Hue, 'Off we go'... potatoes, frozen chips (15 bags) tomatoes, water, cartons of juice, apples, strawberries, oranges, beans, peas, carrots, ice cream, honey, jam, bread, etc etc .....again the endless shopping list quickly began to fill up the two trolleys.

We passed at an electric pace through the tills where the checkout staff quickly scanned the items and threw them back into the trolleys....another 200 euros.

The van was almost full now with the morning's shop as we headed off further into Fuengirola. This time Mercadona, yet another bloody supermarket.

'Not much left, just a few things ..better quality here..' said Hue. Avocados, chicken, mincemeat, beef burgers, salmon, brie and mozzarella cheeses all started to fill up yet another trolley.

'Make sure the avocados are soft or Hamed will not be happy. Always squeeze the avocados', laughed Hue.

My pace slowed as we headed back to the van for the final time. The shopping was complete, it was 1pm and I had not had a coffee since I set off this morning.

We pulled illegally onto the pavement on the promenade in the van beside a fairly busy cafe as this was the nearest place to park for the restaurant which was pedestrianised.

'Go and get the trolley. I will wait here', said Hue.

I rushed to the restaurant about 50 metres away, where the two Barbaras were busy cleaning to pick up the trolley. The two maintenance guys were just finishing off re-plastering the ceiling.

Much to the amusement of the people in the cafe I made four of five trips from the van to the restaurant feeling very conspicuous filling and emptying the trolley after each trip onto the bar and restaurant floor.

On my last trip to the car I noticed that a police car had pulled up alongside the Berlingo for a little chat about our parking. Much more to come on this one.

Hue apologised to the police and pulled away from the front heading towards the safety of his garage.

'Where the hell are we going to put this lot'? I said as I walked back into the restaurant for the last time. The two girls were looking in astonishment at the piles of shopping strewn around the floor and covering the top of the bar.

Luckily Hue arrived back and took us all through the various fridges, freezers, shelves and cupboards scattered around the place to hide everything away.

'We've got the fish and beer, still waiting for the gas' said my wife, Barbara. 'The San Miguel chap gave us this card to sign for every delivery. We get twenty percent cash back every December on all orders placed with them. Keep it safe'.

'I need a coffee, I'm knackered, are you coming?' I asked the two Barbaras.

At that point Hamed entered the restaurant smiling.

'Pechuga (lettuce) I forgot pechuga'. Go back to Eroski its nearest..we need six'. Shit I thought as I headed back towards the supermarket trying to figure out the route.

'I'll see you tonight at 5', said Hue as I left the restaurant.

15 minutes later I arrived back with the six missing lettuces and immediately headed for the cafe with my wife and sister. Hamed agreed to watch out for the gas man.

We sat down in the cafe and ordered coffee and sandwiches.

'We need a car, there is no way I can do this without a car', I said quite concerned.

After a quick bite we headed back to the restaurant.

Hamed was busy in the kitchen with Halima, prepping for the evening ahead.

'I'll do the lasagne', my sister Barbara offered to Hamed.

Hamed nodded as Barbara entered the kitchen which had suddenly sprung into life. The oven rings were all full of massive pans bubbling away, the ovens were firing ahead at full blast and Hamed was slicing the huge slabs of meat into separate portions while at the same time mixing a variety of sauces. The kitchen was hot, very, very hot as my sister dug out a large tray ready to make the lasagne. Within a few minutes she was obviously struggling a bit and becoming very, very warm in the heat of the kitchen.

Hamed was looking on concerned and said.

'I will finish, you can go now'.

We all watched as Hamed took over and constructed the huge 20 portion lasagne in a matter of minutes adding the various cartons of cream and tomato flavours as he went, ready for the oven. Hamed was very impressive and obviously did not need any help much to the relief of my sister Barbara.

'Gas, we need gas. You will have to find the truck, it will be around somewhere', shouted Hamed. 'Take the trolley, go, go, quick'.

I wandered into the street with the empty supermarket trolley and noticed a few newly supplied gas bottles outside other restaurants.

Pointing to a bottle I shouted across to a waiter in one of the restaurants, 'Where is the gas man?'

He pointed back towards the front and I raced down the street with the trolley with 3 empty gas bottles.

About 100 metres along the front I could see the wagon and was feeling a bit conspicuous as I passed the tourists wandering along the front with my shopping trolley.

I shouted to the gas man 'Tres', pointing to the bottles in my trolley and holding up three fingers.

He stopped and exchanged the empty bottles for full ones, handing over another 60 euros.
Feeling self satisfied I walked back to the restaurant where Hamed was stood panicking beside the door.

He grabbed the first bottle and rushed towards the small room behind the kitchen where he connected the full bottle as if his life depended on it.

'Just in time', he said as I dragged the other two bottles into the store.

I was becoming tired now and we had not even started working the restaurant.

Rafael, George's gopher, appeared at the door.

'Are you ready to go to the Ministerio del Trabajo?', (Employment Office) 'We need to change the work contracts for Hamed, Halima and Everaldo into your name'.

'Can we do this tomorrow morning, it is half past three and we open at five?' I asked. To be honest I had had enough for one day by now and we were not even open for business.

'OK I'll pick you up tomorrow morning at 11', said Rafael, and off he went.

The three of us left the restaurant and headed back to the apartment for a quick shower and change ready for our big opening night.

Robbie called to make sure everything was going to plan.

'Yes great, I'm knackered', I replied.

'By the way do you know any good waiters?' as I remembered that effectively Everaldo would be managing the service by himself. Even though there were three of us there we had zero experience or Spanish linguistic skills which I guessed would be useful in a Spanish restaurant.

'Hang on I'll call you back in a sec', said Robbie as he hung up the phone.

In less than a minute the phone rang again. It was Robbie.

'Sarah, my daughter will do it, she has some experience and can speak a little Spanish. When do you want her?'

'10 minutes', I said, 'We open at 5'.

'Ok, she'll be there at half past', said Robbie.

Washed and changed we headed back to the restaurant where Everaldo was busy setting up the tables on the terrace for the night ahead.

'Hola' he greeted us. 'We need sal (salt)'.

For the third time that day I headed back to Eroski this time to buy salt.

When I returned Everaldo was teaching the two Barbaras the table numbers and how to write out the orders (3 copies), one for the chef, one to be hung on the wall outside the kitchen and one to sit on the bar. Each order had to be coded with an (M) for menu del dia or (C) for a la carte with obviously the table number written at the top. Drinks were added at the bottom of the sheet.

All orders had to be verbalised to the chef in case of any questions before he accepted the paper order.

When we heard the chef shout what sounded like 'Sally' from the kitchen that meant that the food was ready to be taken to the table.

Next, drinks training, three large ice cubes in a narrow glass then count to six while pouring from the bottle to impress the customers.

'The short looks as if the glass is full which pleases the British' he said. In reality he amount used is very small….so clever'.

He then demonstrated everything from cutting lemons to making sangria.

Finally, the coffee machine showing us how to make cappuccino, americano, latte, espresso, cortado, drambuie, baileys and tia maria flavoured concoctions and some specific Spanish coffee variations which we had never heard of.

Meanwhile Hue and Sarah the waitress came into the restaurant, just as the first customer arrived.

Having just managed to take off her coat to be introduced to everyone, Everaldo called to her.

'Follow me and watch', said Everaldo to Sarah, obviously putting his authority in place early. They headed towards the first customers with the menus.

The three of us watched from behind the bar, the barrier making us feel safe away from real customers while the orders were taken.

Everaldo returned and headed behind the bar with Sarah which was now becoming quite crowded.

He poured two draft beers and then made an extravagant display of pouring two bacardi and cokes tipping the bacardi into the glass with his hand held about one metre above the glass.

'Count for six seconds while you pour', said Everaldo. 'Don't worry not much bacardi comes out of the bottle spout'.

'Right Phil', said Hue, 'I'll take you through this list'.

He produced a list of suppliers and telephone numbers and explained the purpose of each service.....

Ice cubes
Knife sharpening
Beer .. San Miguel

Beer other
Soft drinks, water and spirits
Water Company
Electric
Gas Bottles
Vegetables delivery service
Fish
Meat..emergency
Fridge, kitchen appliance maintenance
Egg man delivery
Till Maintenance
Pest Control

'Now the till', he said.

I busily scribbled notes as he took me through the various buttons before moving onto the more complex tasks.

.....changing till roll
.....changing prices
.....changing names
.....end of day print

etc, etc

My brain was now overloaded and I pulled a beer for the first time to relieve the stress.

He then picked up the remote control for the combined heating and air conditioning system and began pressing buttons to show me the operation. Things had now stopped going into my memory bank and I just nodded to him pretending that I understood.

At that point I looked up and noticed about five or so tables busy. Everaldo was striding around in his element with Sarah desperately trying to keep up having received clear instructions that her job was just to clear the plates while Everaldo took all orders and served the customers.

The first bill arrived back at the till to process. It was a debit card.

'Shit' I said, 'Do we have a card machine?'

Hue took control and showed me the machine hidden on a shelf behind the bar.

'Where will the money go?' I said nervously to Hue. I hadn't even considered this.

'Have you not changed it with the bank?' said Hue.

'No' I replied, 'Didn't cross my mind'.

'Then the money will go to George's account', he said.

I sheepishly wandered over to a table and for the first time actually spoke to a real customer with an apology and a lie.

'The machine isn't working', I said.' Do you have any cash?'

'No problem', they replied and handed over a 100 euro note. The disaster was averted for now as I made a note that I must go to the bank in the morning to link the card machine to my business account.

I went back to the till with Hue supervising.

'Right', he said, 'Off you go'.

My brain had now stopped functioning as I looked back at my scribbled notes which made no sense to me.

'Can we go through the till buttons again?' I said.

'OK, no problem' said Hue. 'But I will have to go in a minute'.

This time I really had to concentrate as Hue went through the whole process again, just as the next bill arrived.

I picked it up and processed the bill correctly even giving the correct change and received an ironic clap from Hue.

'Well done', he said.

Hue then printed out from the credit card machine the details of the account, merchant-id etc and told me to give it to the bank to do the transfer into my name.

'See you tomorrow at 5 for more training', said Hue as he left the restaurant.

'Tell customers that the machine isn't working when they sit down...only cash for tonight', I said to Everaldo and Sarah.

The evening passed in a blur. I spoke to one of the customers who had been watching the proceedings in front of him with interest and was apparently a regular at the Dom Miguel.

'Just started?' he said.

'Can you tell, first night', I replied.

Obviously, referring to myself and the two Barbaras he said. 'You all look very busy but not very organised and not actually achieving much', he laughed. 'Food still good though, apart from the frozen vegetables'.

This was the second time I had heard this comment and feeling brave mentioned to Hamed, the chef, that two different parties had said this to me about the frozen veg.

Hamed replied, ' No, No...mix of frozen and fresh..we mix the two'.

'Can we do just fresh from now on?' I said.

'OK, OK', replied Hamed not looking too happy.

The end of the evening's service was heralded by Hamed appearing out of the kitchen for the first time to load the shopping trolley with 2 full bags of leftovers ready to be dumped at the underground rubbish dump on the promenade.

We placed a large bag of empty bottles on top of the rubbish in the trolley.

'Come with me I show you', said Hamed and we wheeled the trolley towards the promenade where there were metal chutes coming out of the pavement to tip the rubbish which ended up in bunkers underneath.

It was now around 1230am.

'You eat now?' said Hamed as we returned to the restaurant.

Out of the kitchen came five meals. It was the first time today we had eaten properly.
The three of us sat down with Everaldo and Sarah and for the first time that day we all relaxed as we devoured our late dinner.

Hamed and Halima breezed past us towards the door, with Hamed passing me a small shopping list as he went by.

'Hasta manana' ...until tomorrow they both shouted across to us as they left. Luckily the shopping list was not too bad with only around dozen items that I had to find ready before the service tomorrow.

Emptying the till of the night's takings the three of us head back to the apartment.

'465 euros less 20 euros float', I said disappointingly considering I must have parted with over 1,200 euros during today.

'So much for George's 1,000 euros a night', I added as we all headed towards our beds for the night.

The next morning I was up at 7am ready for the two kilometre hike to the bank in Los Boliches.

I was first in the queue when the bank opened and I headed towards the counter.

'I need to transfer this credit card payment service and link it to my account straight away', I said, as I handed them the printout from the till.

The teller asked for my NIE number and I explained that the solicitor was arranging this in the next week or so.

'OK', she said. 'Two days, it will be done for you ready for Saturday but don't forget let me have your NIE as soon as you get it'.

I left the bank and headed back to the restaurant where the two Barbaras were busy bleaching the tiled floor and terrace and cleaning the toilets.

Rafael arrived at the door.

'You ready. Let's go to the Ministerio de Trabajo to sort out the work contracts'.

'Let me show you first, Hamed's contract is for 10 hours a week, Halima and Everaldo's are for 20 hours. Don't worry it is just for them to pay less tax. They work much more than this for you'.

'OK', I replied, 'Whatever, let's go'.

We jumped into Rafael's car and headed for the Ministerio de Trabajo. We pulled up outside an official looking building which had queues forming outside the door.

We waited our turn patiently and moved inside the building where literally hundreds of people, mainly Spanish, were congregated all very agitated and very loud.

My head was beginning to hurt from the racket as we reached the front of the queue.

An official took us through into another office with five or six desks all covered in papers, however the noise level even in there did not abate by a single decibel.

Rafael handed the papers to the clerk and explained what we were looking to do.

'OK', the clerk smiled and said 'Mr Rogers, NIE number please', in very good English.

I explained the situation to the clerk who said. 'OK I can do temporary transfer...three weeks only. You must bring me your NIE number when you get it or they cannot work in the restaurant for you'.

He stamped some papers all written in Spanish and asked me to sign, not understanding a jot what I was signing up to.

I duly signed the papers, received a copy and we left the madhouse.

'You want a car?' Rafael piped up. 'This one is for sale... brand new engine fitted last month. Hue forgot to put any oil in and the engine blew up...you want to drive back?'

'OK', I replied as I jumped into the driver's side.

The van seemed to be in reasonable condition and offered what I thought was a fair price for a four year old vehicle.

'2,500 euros cash', I said to Rafael.

Rafael immediately phoned George to tell him of the offer.

'George wants 5,000 euros', said Rafael.

'No chance', I replied which ended the conversation.

On arriving back at the Dom Miguel I immediately rang Henrique, the abogado to discuss the need for the NIE numbers for the Employment Office and Bank. After all he was charging me 400 euros to sort out the three NIE's for myself Steve and Liam. Rafael had also informed me that all invoices from suppliers and other general receipts for accounting purposes would have to have my NIE number printed and this increased the urgency for this to be sorted.

I spoke to Natalia, his assistant who took the message and promised that Henrique would ring me later that afternoon.

It was approaching 3pm now and again I was feeling ready for a sleep.

'Going back to apartment now to have quick kip', I said to the two Barbaras. 'Will be back at 5'.

'OK, see you then. We will go and get ready when you get back here', my wife, Barbara replied.

I walked back to the apartment, dropped on the bed and within seconds was fast asleep.

I was awoken by my sister Barbara shaking me to wake up.

'Quick, get up, get up!!!', she shouted.

'What the fuck?' I mumbled still three quarters asleep.

'Get up, we have had an accident at the restaurant', she said.

I jumped up now wide awake, 'What's happened?'

'A little boy has run into the menu pedestal and has a huge bruise on the side of his head', she continued.

'Is he OK?' I said.

'Yes he's OK but his father isn't. He's going to the police to report that the menu pedestal was too far out into the street and get us shut down. By the way he is completely pissed. He is having a right go at Everaldo... I think he's going to hit him'.

'He wants to speak to you and is coming back in fifteen minutes'.

I got dressed and quickly walked back to the Dom Miguel feeling apprehensive. This was our second day....great.

Back at the restaurant, Everaldo was looking a bit frightened.

'What has he said to you?' I asked Everaldo.

'He is saying that I called his son a 'pero' (dog). I didn't do anything of the sort, in fact it was me who put a bag of ice on the kids head', said Everaldo.

'OK, leave it with me', I said just as what looked like a typical British yob came lumbering down the street, obviously quite drunk. His face was red with rage as he came towards the restaurant pulling his son behind him. To be honest his son looked absolutely fine.

'I'm going to the fucking police', he shouted. 'This pedestal shouldn't be in the street...and as for that bastard, pointing to Everaldo who was stood behind the bar. I speak Spanish, he called my son a dog'.

'Look, we are all very sorry for what happened to your son, it was obviously an accident. He seemed to be running down the street not looking where he was going', I replied.

'I'm going to get a denuncia from the police' he slurred, 'to get you closed down'.

Denuncias are a throwback to when the Germans invaded Poland for the Polish people to shop their neighbours in return for favours from the gestapo. These were still rife in Spain whose legal system still operates in the dark ages.

'Look we are sorry, I have known Everaldo for ages (I lied) and there is no way he would say anything like that'.

'What can we do, we have only just opened?' I said. 'Do you want a free meal or a drink? What do you want us to do?'

The yob continued to repeat his threats to the point where there was no point in trying to either pacify or communicate with him.

'Look', I said, 'It was an accident. I can't see the point of carrying on this conversation'. I was becoming a little angry with him now.

'I'm going to the police', he repeated again.

My patience had now reached the end.

'Well why don't you just piss off there then and get out of my restaurant. Just go'.

My wife, sister and Everaldo looked on in horror and pulled me slightly away from him as the yob stepped back towards the wall behind him.

'Look we are all very sorry', said my sister. 'But you had better just go now'.

The yob moved back towards the door and out onto the street shouting for his son to follow.

'Right,' I said, 'I will go and get changed now', and walked back to the apartment.

The night in the restaurant provided more coaching from Everaldo and I was becoming a little more confident using the till and serving drinks, making coffee and using the glass washing machine.

Everaldo taught us everything from how to hold and serve 3 plates with only two arms to folding the napkins in the shape of a shell, not that we were ready to actually serve real customers.

Hue came back for a short while to test me on what he had demonstrated the previous evening. We again went through the till and air conditioning processes before he left.

Regularly a number of Chinese girls selling tat and black Africans apparently from Asda's international lucky, lucky department selling watches and dvd's would begin to mingle with the customers on the terrace. However, as soon as they ventured one metre inside the restaurant they were greeted by Everaldo.

'Fuera, fuera, out, get out', he shouted and they slowly moved back to the terrace.

The street was also awash with musicians with accordions and violins creating a horrendous din and generally annoying customers, who again had a habit of moving into the restaurant with their caps to collect money after their performances.

They were greeted with the same message by Everaldo.

The main customers in the restaurant were British and Irish with a smattering of Scandinavians and Spanish and I occasionally ventured from behind the bar seeking feedback on the meals we were providing.

Now and then a number of suppliers entered the restaurant selling their wares with offers to deliver. Vegetables, the egg man, laundry services, drinks suppliers a guy selling plants etc etc, I took their cards, just in case.

The main issue at this point affecting the harmony of running the restaurant was Sarah.

Nicknamed 'The Slug' by Everaldo she appeared to be in a semi comatose state most of the time with her face glued to her mobile and this was affecting the service big time. He was not happy.

At this point in time Everaldo due to his obvious knowledge was someone we had to keep on side and at the end of service as Sarah left the restaurant he came towards me behind the bar.

'Sarah go now or I go', he said 'She is no good, like a slug. She stay, you pay me more', he said, knowing that he had us over a barrel.

'Ok, I will sort it out', I said.

The night ended as before with a meal and disappointment. 300 euros tonight taken. Not good.

I sat down with Hamed before he left. I was paying Hamed 1,500 euros per month and even after two days was becoming a little worried.

'Hamed, George told me 1,000 euros a night, easy, we have just made 300, what is going on'. I said.

'George clever businessman', he smiled and followed this up with 'You make your money in the summer'.

I actually found out later that Hamed had not actually worked a summer at the Dom Miguel.

Solicitors and Shopping

The situation between Everaldo and Sarah had now reached crisis point and they had stopped communicating altogether. Her nickname 'the slug' to be honest was quite apt and Everaldo had a point. Myself and the two Barbaras were now also beginning to venture onto the floor to speak to customers and help clear and reset tables. Confidence was increasing slowly.

On the following Tuesday, early evening, while preparing the restaurant a beautiful, blonde Swedish girl called Eva appeared at the door obviously spotted by Everaldo whose face lit up.

'She wants a job', Everaldo piped up excitedly.

We all gathered round her as she took us through her experience of waitressing in the past. She could also speak many languages.

'Certainly get the guys in', we all thought, as we asked her how soon she could start.

'Now if you want', she replied.

'Great, can you start tomorrow, we open at five', I said, thinking how to break the news to Sarah.

'OK, see you then', she replied as we all looked at each other thinking how lucky this find could be.

At the end of service that evening I told Sarah that she was sacked. The start of many more to follow.

The next day I got a call from the Employment Office asking about the NIE numbers.

'We need the numbers now, or you will have to close', they said.

I had not heard from Natalie or Henrique the solicitor who had promised to call me back and I called their office again.

Natalie answered. 'Has Henrique not called you?' she said. 'He is out at the moment. I will make sure he does when he gets back'.

I explained the threat from the Employment Office to her and ended the call with 'Make sure he does'.

It was now late afternoon and still no contact from Henrique and I started to become worried so rang again. This time no answer, they were closed.

Next day I rang Natalie first thing and this time really lost it.

'What the hell am I paying you for? I can't employ anyone, the bank and employment office are chasing me ..I can't do any bloody accounts because my invoices will not be accepted. You have promised to ring me twice now. Sort this out now !!!...'

'Don't worry', she said.

'Don't worry, I replied I have never dealt with such a shambles of a company as yours....you are a bloody disgrace and I don't want you lot to manage the Boxto sale I'll go somewhere else. Sort out the NIE numbers now or the place will be bloody well closed down'.

'Another question, have you transferred the utility services yet and if not, why not?' I said curtly.

'No, not yet I will do this today', she replied.

'Right, get Henrique to call me in the next 10 minutes. Do you understand?' I said angrily.

'Ok,ok', she said.

In less than one minute my phone rang it was Henrique sounding very serious.

'They will not close you down', he said. 'I will come and see you this afternoon and we can sort this out'.

The stress of the last few days was now beginning to take its toll with me and when Henrique turned up at the restaurant I was still furious.

'Right, why have the NIE numbers not been done?' I started.

'We would need to send someone from the office to the Oficina de Extranjeros (Foreign Office building) to sort this out for you in Fuengirola', said Henrique. His office was based near Puerto Duquesa around twenty miles away.

'None of my staff are available to do this, but here are some forms I have brought you can go yourself', he continued.

'So that's it, you can't really be bothered', I said.

'No, very busy, it is simple to do', he replied.

'OK then if you are so busy I am assuming that you have no time to sort out the Boxto contract then', I said curtly.

'No, no we can still do that', he replied.

'No thanks, finish the services direct debit transfers and setups and that is all I want you to do. Natalie said they will be done by tomorrow or is that another false promise', I said.

'No, it will be done today, I will make sure off it', said Henrique.

'OK, send me the bill for what you have actually done. I make it 2,300 euros in total. Is that correct?'

Henrique studied the quotation that he had sent to me. 'That is correct', he agreed.

We shook hands and he left the restaurant.

As soon as he had gone, I wandered down to the restaurant three doors away called Raw which was being run by an English couple, Barry and Karen.

I introduced myself and they had already seen me flying around the last few days.

After brief pleasantries, I asked. 'How did you get your NIE numbers, did you do it yourself?'

'No chance', they laughed. 'We went to the Oficina de Extranjeros with our solicitors assistant. It took about three hours to sort out. Thank god they were there to be honest', said Karen. 'It's a madhouse'.

'Do you think you could have done it yourself? My solicitor has just given me these papers to take to sort out myself', I said showing them the papers.

'No way' they said' 'Get a solicitor quick. You need NIE numbers to do everything over here...even farting', they laughed.

'Think I may have upset my solicitor', I replied.

'Don't worry, they said, if you need anything just come and see us. Happy to help. We have just been here ourselves for 6 weeks and learned a bit about how this place operates', said Karen.

I walked back to the restaurant needing to think fast to sort this out.

I rang David, from Spanish bars, who was the agent looking after the Boxto sale.

'David I have a problem', I started, before telling him that I had got rid of the abogado who was until twenty minutes ago was looking after the sale.

'Don't worry', he said. You can use Antonio from Británico Associates, he is a great guy. I used him when I bought my own restaurant here four years ago. He is also the abogado the Boxto owners are using as well so will be cheaper. His office is five minutes away, do you want me to ring him and make an appointment for tomorrow?'

'OK thanks, let's do that', I replied without thinking, not crossing my mind that using the same solicitor as the sellers may not be the brightest idea I had ever had. Anyway anything to remove another problem.

The next day I went to see Antonio in his office in the centre of Fuengirola.

David was right, what a charming guy. He was about 45 years old and must use the same tailor as Henrique..immaculate from head to foot.

Antonio told me about his younger days, when Boxto was always the highlight of his weekends and what a great place it was.

'Great bar, great business', he said, 'You will do very well there. Have you got a gestor by the way?' A gestor is someone who looks after all types of paperwork on behalf of stupid foreigners like myself including tax returns.

'No', I replied. 'It hasn't crossed my mind'.

'We have Carlos, best in Spain, let me introduce you', he said.

We walked down the corridor and entered a busy office with 4 desks stacked with paperwork.

From behind one of the piles appeared Carlos, a smart, young chap about 30 who spoke excellent English. Little did I know at this point that Carlos would turn out to be my best friend for the next two years.

'OK', said Antonio, 'Do you want to use Carlos and let me handle the new contract?'

'Yes', I said, 'Can you give me your prices, I will need you to manage the service charge transfers as well for the electricity, water and landline?'

'By the way there is something urgent I need', I continued. 'NIE numbers, I need them yesterday'.

'I agree. You do need them straight away', confirmed Antonio, turning to Carlos speaking in Spanish.

'I can sort this out with you on Friday', said Carlos. 'I go to the Oficina de Extranjeros anyway, every Friday. Meet me there at 9am and we will get this done straight away'.

'Fantastic', I replied.

Antonio walked to the far end of the office to speak to one of his female staff.

He returned in five minutes. 'OK Phil, I will have costs by Monday. I will include costs for Carlos. It will be a monthly charge for managing your accounts and many other things to help you. Come into the office at 2pm and Stella, one of my legal assistants will explain them to you'. He waved across the room to Stella who smiled and nodded back to him.

I left the office feeling ecstatic on such a high I even thought I could begin taking orders in the restaurant. 'Well maybe not yet', I said to myself.

Antonio and Carlos seemed to have sorted out my main problems.

Meanwhile the restaurant seemed to be running a little better. Everaldo was running around trying to impress Eva who herself was very capable and had the added advantage of tempting the guys into the restaurant.

The takings over the next few days were all over the place ranging from 200 to 650 euros and we still had not managed to crack the 1,000 euro figure.

Even in the short time we had been there couples on a week or two week holiday started to return, I think more to see how we were doing and hoping for some entertainment watching us struggle. I took the liberty at this point to start taking some food orders from the returning couples, which I found not to be as hard as I had thought.

The main reason was to solicit feedback and it was obvious that the meals we were serving were excellent.

Hamed was a great and experienced cook, with his speciality being the fantastic range of sauces he provided for the different meats and fish. Honey & lemon, cream and mushroom, pepper sauces as well as specialities such as Béarnaise sauce. He also produced excellent paellas as well as freshly prepared pasta and lasagne and a range of desserts which changed daily.

I racked my brains trying to figure out why some nights could be reasonably busy and others poor. I guess I would be a millionaire if I was able to crack this one and sell on the solution to all restaurant owners.

One day just before service I spoke to Hamed about the variation in customer numbers asking for his advice.

He replied...'Quarter full equals full'.

'What do you mean?' I replied.

'Get the restaurant a quarter full always.....talk to customers looking at the menu, offer them free wine....anything just to get them in. When restaurant is quarter full others will see we are busy and follow, especially the Brits. Easy, you are now full'. Waiters to be honest for who Hamed had little regard anyway are lazy. 'They just sit around waiting for customers to come in. No good, very lazy. Also, sit them at these tables to start off with, pointing to the 4 tables just inside the door. It makes the restaurant look more busy....easy'.

It took me a while to accept what Hamed was saying and I wandered down the street past the other restaurants. Most had waiters outside talking to customers.

'By the way, big shop tomorrow', he said and he pulled out a huge list similar to the one given to Hue the week before. I needed a car.

'I have to meet with the gestor tomorrow to sort out my NIE number', I replied.

'No food, no restaurant. You must shop', said Hamed.

After considering what Hamed had told me at the end of the night I sat down with Eva and Everaldo with Hamed positioned within hearing distance.

'I want you to talk to customers, looking at the menu before they continue walking down the street and get them in here'.

'No', said Everaldo, 'I am a waiter. I take orders and serve the food and drinks'. Eva just nodded back to me, just to humour me more than anything I think.

'Just try it', I asked again, 'Just for the first hour until we have a number of tables full at the beginning of the evening'.

'We'll see', said Everaldo, 'I am a good waiter, this should not be my job'.

He was just beginning to annoy me now and it registered that I must make it a priority to stop being dependent on him as soon as possible.

They left for the evening leaving me unsure as to how successful my request had been.

Hamed raised his eyebrows knowing that my efforts had been in vain and said,' Hasta manana' as he reached the door.

Friday morning arrived and at around 8' o'clock I squatted outside of a car rental shop waiting for it to open. At 08.45am the owner arrived and I quickly sorted out a car ready for my first big shop on my own.

By 9am I was in the car and driving quickly to the Oficina de Extranjeros to meet up with Carlos to sort out my NIE number.

The place was crammed with hundreds of people and we pushed through the crowd to pull a ticket from a dispensing machine. We were number 96 and displayed in each corner of the huge office on black units with red led's was the number 5.

'First get photographs, there is a machine outside. You need four. Then go for a coffee', said Carlos. I have lots to do here. Come back in two hours and it will be our turn. Leave your phone switched on, just in case and don't go too far'.

I left the office and wandered over to queue for the photo booth to sort out my photographs for the impending NIE meeting. I then wandered into a cafe next door full of people holding their tickets.

After three coffees, and two hours of studying the shopping list, I was becoming more and more confused. Chicken..Mercadona or was that Lidl. Anchovies Macro..no Lidl. The only thing that I could remember for sure was that I had to shop at Carrefour for the wine, but I couldn't remember the directions to get there. I was becoming more and more anxious by the second.

After two hours I returned to the Oficina de Extranjeros and saw Carlos standing by the door.

'Number 89, seven to go', he said.

After another agonising half an hour gazing at the number displays it finally clicked onto number 96.

Carlos raced off through the crowd of people towards one of the office doors.

'Come, come quickly', he shouted.

We entered a room and sat at a desk while Carlos started speaking to one of the clerks who he appeared to know very well from lots of previous visits.

'Give me the photos and passport', demanded Carlos.

He handed these to the clerk who quickly checked the documents and stamped two pieces of paper.

'You sign', requested the clerk, and I quickly scribbled my signature as requested.

'There you go Mr Rogers, your new NIE number', said the clerk.

I felt that a huge weight had now been lifted from my shoulders as I said goodbye to Carlos and thanked him for helping me out.

'How do I get to Malaga from here?' I said to Carlos. 'Need to do the shopping'.

He gave me brief directions and I raced back to the car. It was now 1230pm.

I jumped into the car and sped off along the main dual carriageway to Malaga, heading for Macro.

'Turn off, one before airport', I kept repeating to myself. 'Cross bridge, rejoin carriageway, Macro on the right'.

After twenty minutes I saw the airport sign and noticed Macro across the carriageway on the other side of the road. I pulled into the inside lane and headed for the carriageway exit. So far so good, over the bridge and back down the other side, pulling off the road down a dirt track and into the Macro car park.

I grabbed a trolley, and rushed towards the meat section which I remembered was towards the top right of the store. The food labels in Macro were all in Spanish as I grabbed my list which Hamed had written in both Spanish and English.

Solomillo...fillet steak, Ternera..sirloin steak, cerdo...pork loin, chuleta de cerdo...pork chops.

I grabbed the large slabs of meat and threw them in the trolley. Chicken, what about the chicken. No that's Mercadona I remembered. Should I get it here just in case I can't find Mercadona? Can I remember how to get to Mercadona?...no better get it where I was told. Shit..where is the cheese and butter?.

I raced up and down the aisles and aisles and found them. I then referred to my other list which I had been scribbling when last here with Hue. Row 47, tinned mushrooms, Row 18, tomatoes, Row 57 olive oil, sugar Row 12. I frantically ticked off what seemed to be a small number of items from the list. Paper tablecloths, red and white pattern, where the fuck were they? Shit!!

It's now 0130pm and we open at 5. I still have three shops to get to and am beginning to panic.

I flew to the checkout showing the teller Hue's Macro card which he had given me and whizzed across the car park and literally threw the food into the boot of the car.

Next Carrefour for the wine. All I remembered was that it was back down the other side of the carriageway, past the airport heading for Malaga.

I headed off in the wrong direction on the carriageway, took the first exit and rejoined the main carriageway going in the opposite direction heading back towards Malaga.

After three miles I could see Carrefour on my right, but there were no easy slip roads to get across to it.

A road was joining me from the right with heavy traffic filtering onto the main carriageway.

'Right, I'll have to go for it', I thought out loud.

I grabbed the wheel tightly and slewed at speed across two lanes of traffic heading for some waste ground from where I hoped I could access Carrefour.

The blaring of horns was horrendous as I cut up about five or six cars moving across the lanes.

I stopped on the waste ground to check that I was still alive and drove over a grass verge to join a service road into Carrefour.

'Yes, I've bloody well done it', I said to myself as I again raced into Carrefour with another trolley.

This time I did not check my list but grabbed 24 bottles of red and white wine plus a few other random bottles which I vaguely recognised and again dashed towards the checkouts. It was now 2.30pm and I had finished about one half of the shopping.

My phone rang, it was my wife Barbara.

'Where are you?' she said.

'Carrefour, nearly in Malaga. Coming back to Fuengirola now, still got Lidl and Mercadona to do. Can't talk need to get going. Will ring you when near the restaurant. Have the trolley ready'.

I headed out of the Carrefour car park and for the fourth time that day rejoined the main carriageway, heading the wrong way towards Malaga.

I was now driving into the city and there were no major junctions coming off the carriageway.

'How the hell do I turn round?' I said to myself, just as I noticed a car ahead pulling into a right hand mini filter lane.

Luckily, at the bottom of the lane were some traffic lights and I headed left cutting back across the main carriageway to rejoin it going in the other direction back towards Fuengirola.

After twenty minutes I pulled into Lidl car park, grabbed the obligatory trolley and rushed into the store, hitting the main vegetable section first. I just grabbed everything in front of me, potatoes, carrots, beans, cabbages, melons, apples, oranges, cauliflowers, ham, cheese, bacon and dumped them in the trolley.

Looking quickly at my list I began to drag boxes of 36 cartons tomato puree and 24 of cream into the trolley followed by cheese, ham, ice cream, profiteroles, chips don't forget the chips (15 bags), honey...3, jam....2, bread, juice cartons....6 etc etc.

It was now 3.45pm as I drove out of Lidl.....one more shop to go, and I grabbed some dry bread and a bottle of water from my stash to eat, having just realised I had had nothing since the cups of coffee this morning.

Mercadona, the final frontier, the final destination, however I was very aware that I did not have everything on the list.

'Don't forget to squeeze the avocados', I laughed to myself as I hit the aisles. Chicken check, mince check, beef burgers check, bread check. Got them .. god it's easy this shopping lark, I said to myself.

I called wife Barbara, 'Back in five minutes. Get down the front with the trolley outside the cafe. We'll have to be quick or the cops will be after us'.

Upon reaching the cafe I quickly threw my first load into the trolley while Barbara guarded the car. I made the dash three times to and from the restaurant spreading everything on the restaurant floor and bar before rushing back to the car and dumping it outside the car rental office.

It was now almost 5pm as Hamed and Halima came into the restaurant to see the carnage.

'Very busy day, yes', laughed Hamed as we all began to move the mountain of food out of sight into various cupboards and freezers.

'How have I done?' I eventually said to Hamed as I passed him back the list.' By the way I could not find the tablecloths in Macro'.

Hamed went through the list beginning to look a little worried.

'No ajo (garlic), coffee, gelatine, pechuga (lettuce), avocados too hard, anchovies, camembert cheese, baked beans, vinegar etc etc.

My face dropped. I was all done in by this point. The first customers started to take an interest in the menu outside.

My wife piped up...' We will go to the Eroski up the road to see if we can find any of this missing stuff', and the two Barbaras set off up the road on their mission.

Hamed could see my disappointment and said, 'I take you next week, show you best meat and what to look for to get the best food, and look for bargains'.

'Thanks', I replied, 'That would be a big help'.

I looked like a tramp after the day I had just had and as soon as Everaldo appeared I made a dash back to the apartment to change ready for the night ahead.

It was not a great night. In fact the pattern of Friday being the worst night for takings became a common theme. I put it down to Friday being the favourite night for either fish and chips or curry, as the Indian restaurant directly opposite the Dom Miguel seemed to thrive every Friday.

The night went off without a hitch although the takings were just around the 400 euro mark.

The weekend continued with the same daily pattern, the only variation being as to whether a 'big shop' was needed or I could get by with a local smaller shop within walking distance.

A routine began to develop. Up at 7am, shopping, back to restaurant, mop and bleach floor, mop and bleach terrace, clean bogs, restock fridges with drinks, refill salt and pepper cellars, refill vinegar olive oil pots, wait for deliveries, eat toast at cafe, back to apartment to iron tablecloths, sleep or sunbathe for 1 hour, shower, change and back to restaurant for the night. Final chore, wash tablecloths before bed. Over the next week a pattern also emerged for the deliveries, Gas Monday and Wednesday, Fish Thursday, San Miguel Tuesday, soft drinks order before 1300pm delivered after 5 the same day. Many other chores interrupted my 1 hour planned sleep which was precious to me. Visiting town hall, sorting out licence, work permits, utility bills, visiting random shops for candles, toothpicks, order pads, stuff for Hamed's kitchen, buckets, mops, tea towels spoons and especially the knives which continually went missing in the restaurant.

On one of my regular visits to Macro I bought some knives which came in packs of three just sellotaped together and placed them in the bottom of my trolley before filling the trolley with the usual mountains of food. Rushing through the checkout as quickly as possible I was loading the food into the car when I noticed the three knives still sat at the bottom of the trolley camouflaged against the silver trolley mesh which I had genuinely not seen or paid for.

This then became a regular occurrence for future visits when for some reason I kept on forgetting they were still in the trolley when checking out. I convinced myself that it was my loyalty payment from Macro, a bit like a nectar card. After all, I was spending about 600 euros a week there. Some weeks I even left them at the bottom of the trolley forgetting to put them in the car which really pissed me off when I realised this back at the restaurant.

On the Monday I met up with Stella from Británico Associates to run through the figures for the Boxto sale due for completion in two weeks on the 1st May.

'My wife won't be in Spain to sign the papers for Boxto, she flies back to the UK on Saturday', I said. 'Can I sign on her behalf?'

'No, no' she replied, 'You must go to Notario, you need Power of Attorney, I will have to take you. We can go on Friday. I will make an appointment for 10 am. Meet me here with your wife, it is not far, we can walk'.

The costs for the Boxto sale were around half of what Henrique's company had quoted so I readily agreed that they could handle the sale.

I then spent the rest of my day off hiking to the bank in Los Boliches, NIE number in hand to officially validate my two accounts. Then on to the Ministerio de Trabajo to legalise my ability to employ staff and finally on the phone to all of my delivery suppliers to make sure that future invoices were printed with my NIE number. Next priority, sort out the NIE with main shops for all future invoices and get my own card for Macro.

The three of us, met for lunch to catch up, especially to discuss how I could manage on my own when the two Barbaras went back home on the Saturday.

'I need a car', I said. 'I will have to start looking around'.

'You need to look at having more deliveries or get Hamed to do the shopping' said my sister, Barbara.

'You can't do that amount of shopping on foot every day', said my wife Barbara

'Good idea, but not too practical. Most of the stuff is from Macro and Lidl and can't be delivered. Maybe I could use a delivery for the vegetables. That would help. I need to organise a hire car to do a massive shop on my day off. Then I could just top up from Eroski and Mercadona just up the road. If I am desperate I could walk to Lidl. There is a second Lidl about one mile away from the restaurant which is closer', I said.

We all agreed.

'You will need an extra large freezer for the big shop' said my sister, Barbara.

We spent the rest of the day and evening introducing ourselves to the other restaurant owners along Fish Alley.

I have already mentioned Karen and Barry, who owned the restaurant called 'Raw' three doors down from where we were who were to become good friends over the next few months as did the guys who ran the Indian directly opposite

We also met Dave and Kate from Salford who ran a small cafe/bar called 'Spanish Sunshine,' up a side street just off Fish Alley.

A guy called Ron who lived in the flat immediately above the Dom Miguel who looked a bit like Ronnie Biggs with long flowing grey hair and his wife Molly came into the restaurant offering consultancy services.

'Been here five years', he said. 'I own the Pig and Parrot pub in the next street. Happy to help you, and save you lots of money', he said.

I later found out to my cost that the beer he served in his pub was so strong to the point that after three pints you were close to being comatose. Obviously the place to go for the Fuengirola alcoholics and the place was full of them.

'I'll give you this for free', said Ron. 'Go and see Eddie down in the port, who owns the Port Bistro Bar. Tell him Ron sent you. He sells litre bottles of all spirits for six euros...proper stuff..no idea where he gets it from'.

'Thanks' I said. 'Any idea where I can get a cheap freezer?'

'Got one in the 'Pig' ...40 euros, come and have a look tomorrow and we can wheel it down to the restaurant', said Ron.

Next door to the Dom Miguel we had 'Little Britain' the smallest bar in the world with two tables outside and one inside run by John and Mary and next to them an English fish and chip shop run by Bill, the most henpecked guy I had ever met and his miserable wife Susan.

All in all there was a villagey feel to the place where the Brits stuck together and helped each other out, especially when someone had run out of food or drink or even gas during the evening.

On the corner opposite there was an off license, which proved to be invaluable for me as my stock levels were not high and I often ran to the shop just to complete a drinks order.

The next evening Tuesday, during service there was a commotion outside the restaurant.

Two official looking guys wandered up to the bar where I was busy serving drinks.

'We are from the Town Hall. You must move chairs outside', they said.

'What?' I replied looking surprised.

'Come with me,' they said and I obediently followed them outside.

'You over the line...chairs over the line', said one of the guys.' You must stay within the lines'.

I noticed that there was a very faint red line which apparently marked out my terrace space and two of the chairs were about four inches over the boundary.

'For god's sake, have you nothing better to do', I uttered.

'They started to get a bit serious. 'You move them now or we close you down', he said.

I picked up the chairs and angrily moved them the necessary four inches.

'Happy now', I said sarcastically.

'We check tomorrow', they replied, and wandered off.

Hamed noticed the proceedings.

'Phil, don't upset these guys. They can make your life very difficult', he said. I certainly found out what he meant later in the month.

The next day I met up with Ron to check out the freezer which was absolutely perfect and we wheeled it down the street over the cobbles into the Dom Miguel. After such a bumpy ride I was astonished that it burst into life when I plugged it in.

Wednesday was big shop day and this time I felt much less stressful as I jumped into Hamed's car with him and we headed off towards Malaga for the Macro shop.

Hamed was an interesting chap and he had certainly been around. We discussed a few small tweaks to the menu, which we agreed but I did not give in on having mixed fresh and frozen vegetables.

We had a quick coffee in the Macro bar opposite the main warehouse and I went to reception to sort out my own Macro card, as I now had my NIE number. They handed me a temporary piece of paper with a barcode stamped on it to use at the checkout until my card was ready the next week.

Hamed guided me slowly around the store, checking his list and pointing things out which weren't on the list this time but we would need in the future for my reference. He also taught me what to look for when selecting the best slabs of meat.

We followed a similar pattern in the three other shops before returning to the Dom Miguel fully loaded.

'You happier now,' said Hamed. 'You are now expert shopper'.

I thanked him for his valuable time as he left me to unpack and store all of the food and drink.

Saturday soon arrived and the two Barbaras packed up early and headed for the station to catch the train to the airport. We had sorted out the Power of Attorney for me to sign the Botxo contract in two weeks the day before they left with Stella, the abogado's assistant.

Steve and Liam were due to join me the next weekend.

We said our goodbyes as they boarded the train to the airport

I was now on my own for the first time.

Boxto

It's the 30th April tomorrow and Steve and Liam were due to arrive ready for the contract signing on the 1st May and prepare for the grand opening of Boxto.

The Dom Miguel restaurant was still just about holding its own with a nightly income of between 300 and 600 euros.

After a month in charge I began to create a set of accounts on my trusty laptop, trying to make some sense of my costs over the last month.

Right, here we go....monthly outgoings.

Rent (2000)
Terrace Tax (100)
Apartment (900)
Electric/water for apartment(40)
Hamed (1500)
Everaldo (1000)
Halima (800)
Eva (800)
Food (3500)....Macro(1500), Lidl (800), Mercadona (220), Carrefour (500).
San Miguel (300)
Costa supplies (other drinks)(400)
Gas(80)
Fish(300)
Accountant (100 estimate)
Electric, phone, water restaurant (150) estimate
Contingency (200)

Total 12,170 euros

Let's now assume we are open for 26 days with takings averaging 470 euros a night.

Total 12,220 euros needed to break even.

Actually, this rough and ready calculation proved to be incredibly accurate going forward based only on my first month in the restaurant.

470 euros became the key number for my nightly income target and after all it was not yet the summer.

Hamed began to let me borrow his car to do the shopping even though I had to walk about 1.5 miles to his apartment to pick it up. This was much better that hiring a car as I could start the 'big shop' much earlier and be back at the restaurant at around 11.30am.

Being on my own my daily schedule was timed to the minute and I managed to slightly improve it. I decided to buy a bottle of rioja and white wine from Macro, Lidl and Mercadona and asked customers at the restaurant to sample and rank them alongside the Carrefour wine. All wine to me tastes the same.

All agreed that the rioja from Lidl and the white wine from Macro were the best even better than the wine from Carrefour. I was really pleased as the costs per bottle dropped to 1.25 euros and 90 cents respectively. Not bad when selling for 11 euros per bottle and no more risking life and limb cutting across the motorway lanes to get to Carrefour. No wonder bars were offering free wine at that price.

The routine became....

Up at 7am, walk 1.5 miles to pick up Hamed's car, arrive Macro 0845 (opens at 9), quick coffee, queue for shop opening..first in (now familiar with route around store) back in car by 0930.

Drive to Lidl, opens 10am, queue up outside store...first in, back in car by 1030. Drive to Mercadona, in and out by 11. Back to restaurant unload. Finish by 11.30, another coffee at cafe on front. Clean restaurant, wait for deliveries, all before 1pm.

Quick snack at Karen or Dave's cafe, back to apartment by 2...sleep for 1 hour...do ironing, wash, change ..out at 5 back to restaurant until we closed at around 12.30am.

With the help of the new freezer I was able to organise the 'big shop' to around 3 trips per fortnight.

This routine was similar every day as even on the days without a car it took just as long on foot to hump four or five bags of food to and from the restaurant from the local supermarkets. Monday night we closed and this normally involved a trip to the 'Pig' to pick up pearls of wisdom from Ron and to suffer his dodgy lager.

I was also becoming more confident in the restaurant taking orders etc but no less stressed when we were empty. Everaldo was showing no initiative in trying to chat up potential customers so more and more I began to try this myself, thinking, 'What's the worst that can happen?'

It was also apparent that Everaldo and Hamed were not best buddies. One night when we were closing a big row kicked off between them.

'Tony Blair, he's a terrorist', shouted Hamed, glaring at Everaldo.

'No, Blair is a good guy, Saddam was an evil man', responded Everaldo.

This exchange of views went on for some time and became very heated.

At the time I was sat listening to this exchange and obviously did not want to antagonise Hamed especially so said nothing. My view at that time was similar to Everaldo's as this was the view of probably the majority of Brits at that time.

Funny how Hamed was proved to be correct about twelve months later when none of the so called weapons of mass destruction were found in Iraq.

Steve and Liam arrived on the 31st ready for the contract signing the next day. They were bubbling with excitement as they dropped off their luggage at the apartment ready for the grand tour of the newly opened Dom Miguel followed by a quick trip to the 'Pig' of course.

I left them to their own devices for the rest of the evening with the message, 'Don't get drunk, we've got a big day tomorrow. You need to come with me to the bank, first thing, to act as my bodyguards to carry the money'.

My wife had arranged to transfer the 55,000 euros into my Spanish bank account earlier in the week to cover the cost of the lease for Boxto.

The next day after a quick coffee and bacon buttie, the three of us headed along the coast for the familiar hike to the bank in Los Boliches.

Christina was waiting and as before ushered us into the back office to count out the cash all in 50 euro notes. After counting the money we left the bank, tightly clutching the bag of dosh and headed for another quick coffee to be ready for the 10.00am meeting with Antonio, the abogado.

We arrived at his office just before 10am and Diego, Rodrigo and Rolando were there already.

Another Spanish chap called Juan was also sitting at the table who introduced himself as the landlord of Boxto who we had to pay the monthly 1,000 euro rent to.

We all exchanged greetings and sat down at a large table with Antonio at the head.

Antonio in both Spanish and English for our benefit took us through the process we were about to follow.

'I will hold the 12,000 euros for the tax which is due in July', said Antonio. This was based on the statement of accounts they had shown us earlier.

Diego and Rodrigo did not seem very happy with this and started to gesticulate and speak loudly. The gist was that they felt that they should keep the money and pay the tax themselves

I was feeling a little uncomfortable at this stage.

'Do you have the invoices for the last tax period to prove your turnover and profit figures', I asked.

'No, not now, no invoices we do not keep them. You can keep the 12,000 euros, you pay the tax,...no problem', said Rodrigo seemingly worried by my request.

Antonio jumped in at this point. 'I will not keep the money, you keep it Phil, although you must remember to pay in July. Carlos will do all of this for you'.

I let this pass and agreed to hand over the 43,000 euros, keeping the 12,000 euro tax balance to pay in July.

It was a few months later when I discovered that their accounts statement was a load of tosh.

Antonio asked us all to sign the lease contract, split the cash three ways between the three amigos and asked them to count it.

Once they were happy, we all shook hands and agreed to meet at Botxo at 2pm to hand over the keys.

At 2pm on the dot we all arrived at Boxto, to do the handover. There were a few other dodgy looking guys hanging around by the door.

Rolando introduced us to Santiago, Danny and Martin who often helped out in the bar when cover was needed or who sometimes carried out a PR role dragging customers from the streets outside into the bar. Also there was a young English guy called Mikey who was the resident DJ. Standing at the back was a huge, mixed race chap called Emero who I guessed correctly was the bouncer.

They explained to us how the bar operated. All customers once approved by the bouncer paid a cover charge of 10 euros to come into the bar and were given an admission ticket. The ticket could be used in exchange for their first drink.

Steve and Liam were huddled around the guys asking if they could work on the coming Friday night.

Payment for the PR guys seemed to be based around being given free drinks when they managed to get customers to buy the 10 euro ticket. They spent most of their nights half cut.

Payment for Emero and Mikey the DJ was around 10 euros per hour. The bar opened from 10 pm till 4 am.

Diego then took Steve and Liam through the stock ordering process and other bits of admin.

'Are you OK? I asked Steve and Liam.

'Yes, all sorted we can open tomorrow, but one of the toilets are broken', said Liam.

I turned to Diego and Rolando, 'You will be helping them?' I asked, as they had promised a few weeks ago.

'Yes, yes, no problem, will be here on Friday', said Rolando.

'What about employment contracts for the guys?'

'No, no as long as Steve and Liam are here, you will not need any. You will know from the other bar owners if the police or Town Hall are checking. Just make sure the guys are this side of the bar when they arrive', said Rolando.

Rodrigo and Diego walked towards me, and Diego piped up, '1,000 euros for the stock'.

This was the first time this subject had been raised.

'Shit', I thought, I didn't plan for this, but responded that I would check the stock and make an offer.

Luckily I had a reasonable knowledge now of how much the beer, wine and spirits were at cost price with my experience of buying drinks for the restaurant.

I quickly counted through the stock items and said to Diego. '600 euros, is what I make this lot to be'.

'No, No, good quality spirits here …1,000 euros', said Diego.

'I haven't seen anything of good quality in the bar apart from two bottles of brandy and one half bottle of malt whiskey. What have I missed?' I said.

'No no', he said as he picked up a couple of bottles of some strange concoctions of which I have never heard.

'Ok, you can keep them', I said. '650 euros is my final offer and that includes fixing the loo before I pay you'.

He went off to talk to his two mates.

'OK, 650 euros agreed. Rodrigo has just rung for a plumber to fix toilet. He will be here in 1 hour', said Diego.

Just before we left Steve had arranged an early 'team meeting' with his new staff at 7pm on the Friday in the bar next door. I remember thinking and laughing to myself at the time that Steve was using his experience of working in Call Centres who love their team meetings.

I handed Liam some cash for his first stock order, telling him to make sure that my NIE number was added to all receipts. Luckily, the only stock Boxto needed was alcohol and cigarettes.

A cigarette machine stood next to the bar which had a key to open the front and a second key for the cash box inside. I agreed with Steve that he would lock the night's takings in the cashbox before he left as it was not a good idea to be carrying large amounts of cash around at 5 in the morning.

The order, give or take was 20 crates of San Miguel and 3 crates of Coronita, coke, fanta, mixers 10 crates, vodka (10 bottles), gin, bacardi, whiskey, brandy , amaretto, tia maria, pernod, some strange concoction to make cheap free shots, lots of red bull and 10 cartons of assorted fags to stock up the machine. That was about it to be honest, the bar did not serve draft beers or lagers. Should be a very simple model for the lads to manage.

The next day was the Thursday before the big opening night on the Friday. Liam and Steve took delivery of the stock and with the help of Mikey, the DJ put everything away in its place.

Steve and Liam went off to buy some cleaning products, again which made me laugh. They bleached the wooden floors, polished the bar, cleaned the glasses and generally made the place very presentable. I was impressed and even the loo had been fixed as promised.

They spent the rest of the day playing the music very loudly and generally having a good time getting to know each other.

Danny and Santiago (both Spanish speaking) popped into Boxto during the early evening and all five of them were hyped up ready to go on the Friday.

It was May the 1st now and Boxto until the summer months only opened Friday and Saturday nights, although Steve and Liam planned to open seven nights a week as soon as possible.

'See you in the restaurant later, you seem to have everything under control', I said as I left them.

'Yes, see you later dad', said Steve although I knew that I would probably not see them again that day.

The next day, before the opening night in Boxto I prepared for my daily routine at 7am and looked in Steve and Liam's bedroom to make sure they were there to be greeted by a musty smell of stale alcohol.

The rest of the day panned out as normal and as usual I was anxiously standing behind the bar in the restaurant waiting for our first customer.

Two gentlemen appeared at the door dressed in suits.

'Are you the owner?' said the older chap.

' Need to check Licencia de Apertura (opening license)', he continued.

'What licence?' I replied, 'I have only been here for four weeks'.

'You need a license to open. You must have one', said the smaller chap. 'You need fire safety, health and safety certificates, food handling certificate ...your staff also'.

Hamed was listening from the hatch into the kitchen.

'George has license', he said.

'I've never seen it', I replied. 'Can I ring George the previous owner', I said to the two chaps.

The taller chap replied,' No good, you need your own, you are now the owner. You need fire certificate by next week also or you will have to close. The health inspector will also arrive soon to check everything else, she will just arrive with no notice'.

'How do I get a fire certificate?' I asked.

'You need to spray all wood, bars, walls, tables chairs with fire resistant chemical and you will get certificate. Next week, we will check again next week', the taller chap said and they both turned and left the restaurant.

'Can you give me two weeks?' I pleaded.

'OK, 2 weeks', he said.

I was now in a state of panic and immediately rang George.

'Have you got a license to open?' I said.

'Yes we have an opening license', replied George.

'Does it include a fire certificate?'

'No, must be new thing, never needed one', said George.

'Shit, that's all I need', I thought.

I made a mental note to ring Antonio my solicitor on the following Monday for some advice.

The night was a typical Friday, really poor takings. 'Fish and chip and curry night', I said to Hamed.' Maybe we should close on a Friday and open Monday', I continued.

'Ok with me, if you want to', he said. 'Friday night off much better for me'.

After service that night and the usual late meal I headed towards Botxo which was about a 400 metre walk along the promenade and up a side street.

It was about 1am as I made my way through the crowded promenade.

'Free drinks, Heavens Sent...free shots all night...Amigos club, half price till 1am ...Keepers Club' were being shouted in my direction as lots of desperate PR's who obviously needed their free drinks to top themselves up accosted me trying to get me to go into their clubs.

I met Danny and a chap called Martin who were trying to charm customers into Boxto.

'How's it going?' I shouted to Danny.

'Not bad, but not enough people out tonight', he replied.

Just then I felt a strong, tight grip on my left arm pulling me off the pavement towards a small shopping complex.

I turned round to see that I was being grabbed by a large jet black girl about 25 years old.

'20 euros, you very lucky, come with me, good time, good time', she said over and over.

I pulled my arm away as best I could. She really was very strong and Danny who had now seen what was going on came over quickly and shouted at the girl to leave me alone.

She let go of my arm as Danny started to speak to her very sternly, waving his arms around as he did so. At this point I noticed around a dozen of these black African 'ladies' accosting every male that passed by along the promenade mainly focusing on tourists who had obviously had a bit to drink.

'Thanks Danny', I said. 'What did you say to her?'

'Don't worry', he laughed. 'I promise this will never happen again to you. Now she understands and will tell her friends....or else', he said.

Over the months from then on I regularly walked the same route to Boxto late at night. From that point on I was greeted with 'Hello Mr Boxto' by the girls as I passed by and never had a single problem.

I arrived at Boxto and was greeted by Emero standing on the terrace outside the bar collecting the 10 euro entrance fees and issuing the tickets.

'Good night?' I asked.

'Very early yet', he replied as I went into the bar.

The bar was reasonably busy and Steve and Santiago were serving drinks to mainly Spanish customers. I was amazed that Steve seemed to have picked up the language so quickly as he was happily taking drinks orders. Liam was standing in the corner with DJ, Mikey learning how the decks worked as incredibly loud music blasted out.

'How's it going? Where are Rolando and Diego?' I said to Steve as I perched on stool at the edge of the bar.

'Great, they did not show up, but we are OK', he replied. He was really hyper. 'If we get really busy, Danny will come behind the bar and help us'.

I was really unhappy about the no show from these guys but not really surprised. I ordered and paid for a coronita and sat and watched the guys in action, feeling a little conspicuous as there weren't many fifty year olds in the place surprisingly.

I left after five minutes as any sort of conversation was impossible and headed back to the apartment for the evening feeling quite happy, apart from the Opening Licence problem.

The next day after checking that Liam and Steve were safely in bed after my chores I headed back to Boxto to get the night's takings from the cigarette machine.

I opened the shutter and walked into the bar. I was faced with absolute carnage. Wading through rubbish and broken glass I made my way to the far end of the bar which was littered with bottles, half empty glasses and cigarette butts, towards the toilets. The toilet floors were flooded and covered with sodden paper. The inside of the basins were blocked with an indescribable, mix of toilet paper and god knows what, especially the ladies.

I moved carefully towards the cigarette machine and opened the cash box. It was empty apart from a few euro coins.

'Good god', I thought, 'I'll kill them. The lazy sods'.

It was now around 2pm and I rushed back towards the apartment and immediately woke up the two guys.

'The place is a bloody tip, where are the takings?' I said to the pair of them.

They both rose from their pits slowly.

'We'll tidy up when we get up. We have till 10 o'clock' tonight', said Steven still half asleep and obviously slightly still quite drunk.

'Where is the money?' I said.

Steve slowly felt around the floor looking for his trousers which were lying crumpled in the corner of the bedroom.

He slowly picked them up and began to throw a procession of crumpled notes onto the bed from different pockets.

'Why didn't you put them in the cigarette box?' I said angrily. 'You should not be walking around this place at 5 in the morning carrying this much cash'.

'Sorry, he said sheepishly. 'I will tonight'.

I gathered up the array of crumpled notes and headed for the lounge to count the takings.

'750 euros', I counted...better than the bloody Dom Miguel. Not bad'.

Liam and Steve entered the lounge and sat down.

'Still need to pay a few of the guys', said Steve.

'And we need to reorder some stuff ready for tonight' said Liam.

'How much do you need?' I said.

'400 euros should be enough' said Liam.

'I need about 200 euros to pay the guys' said Steve.

I took 100 euros from the pot and handed them back the rest. I needed to find 1,000 euros a month to pay the rent on Boxto and around 200 to cover the service costs.

Liam stood up.

'Have to get to the bar and sort out what we need to order', he said and headed for the door as Steven collapsed on the sofa.

'Make sure you are there at 5 to help Liam tidy up', I said to Steve.

'Ok, ok, don't worry', said Steve.

'I'll get changed now and give Liam a hand before I go to the restaurant', I said, 'Make sure that you are there for 5', I repeated, 'You need to help Liam clear up the bloody mess'.

Before opening the restaurant I checked on the state of Boxto and met Steve, Liam and Mikey all busily clearing the piles of rubbish from the night before.

'Get the guys to tidy up when you close', I said. The place will stink of stale beer if you leave it all day. Go and get some air freshener before you open tonight'.

'Ok', said Liam who still looked tired from the night before.

'And make sure you put the takings in the cigarette machine', I said just as the wagon arrived bringing the evenings drinks ready for the night's action.

On the Sunday morning I returned to Boxto and found the place reasonably clean with 800 euros in crumpled notes stuffed in the cigarette machine cash box. I thought to myself, maybe this place will be lucrative over the summer when we open every day.

Sundays in Fuengirola are not very shopping friendly to say the least. Nothing opens and as for what seemed like their weekly fiestas where I often found the main shops all closed again. It drove me crazy. I spent the rest of the Sunday looking to find items to cover Hamed's daily shopping list.
Wandering around the streets I found one or two mini markets open and managed to find some of the items I needed. I was half expecting to have to beg and borrow stuff from the other restaurants when I saw Dave from the Spanish Sunshine cafe/bar coming towards me.

'Hi Dave, how's it going', I said. 'Any idea where I can get any of this stuff, mainly vegetables?'

'Follow me', he replied as he led me down a sidestreet.

There on the corner was a fruit and vegetable shop which was quite busy.

'This place makes a fortune on a Sunday', said Dave. 'Only place open'.

Outside the shop on display in big baskets was a stack of vegetables which were all obviously way past their sell by date.

'Get all of their stuff out of the bins. Make a fortune every Sunday', laughed Dave

'You're not bloody kidding', I replied as I tentatively started digging among the overripe fruit and vegetables.

'Hamed, will not be pleased', I said to Dave, as I tried to pick the produce which looked just about edible.

I went to the counter with Dave to pay, loaded with potatoes, tomatoes, beans and various other items.

'70 euros', the lady said.

'What for this shit', I replied.

Si, si...you want or no', she replied. Dave was beside himself laughing.

I had no choice as I handed over the 70 euros to the thieving sod behind the counter, determined never to get caught out again, although I was quite a few times over the next few months.

Another of the interesting shops I discovered while touring the streets was a small store called 'Spainsburys'. This was a shop full of all British brands like Heinz, Colmans, Cadbury's etc.

It was a godsend to me as I had already been asked by customers many times for Colman's mustard for steak and mint sauce for the lamb and had to explain they did not have it over in Spain.

I read years later that Sainsburys in the UK were taking legal action against them for 'copying' their name. I think that Sainsbury's legal chaps must have a lot of time on their hands.

I also came across Big Willey's, a British butcher's shop a short distance from the restaurant. This butcher's was well known in Fuengirola and I decided after talking to Hamed to start changing the menu a little. We added Big Willey's pork and pork and apple sausages to the menu with mash, and also added spare ribs which came pre-sealed in individual portions swimming in a fantastic barbecue sauce (two minutes in the microwave and they were done).

I advertised the sausages on the menu as Big Willey's and they became a firm favourite and a great talking point to drag wavering customers into the restaurant.

Willey, the guy who owned the shop gave me a good discount for the reasonably large orders I gave him was also a customer of mine, but he never ordered his own sausages. I still to this day wonder why.

That night just before service I could hear a lot of muttering in Arabic coming from the kitchen between Hamed and Halima.

'You Ok?' I enquired.

Hamed did not reply. He was busy rummaging through the vegetables, half of which went straight into the bin.

'This is shit', he kept commenting in English, at what I had managed to buy from the dustbin shop. He really was very unhappy.

'Sorry', I replied nervously as I walked back to the bar.

The next day, Monday, was my day off, and I went straight to Antonio's office to see if he was available to help me with my threat of closure from the town hall.

Luckily, I managed to grab Carlos who took me into his office.

'Right, Phil, you need a license, to serve food and drink', said Carlos. 'Fire safety certificate is the most urgent. You must have this straight away'.

'What is it?' I asked.

'All wood in the restaurant needs to be treated to make it fire resistant. Then they give you certificate', said Carlos.

'The place is 90 percent wood I said, even the walls', I said. 'Who does it and how much?' I enquired.

'Companies authorised by Fire department, here are two contacts in Fuengirola', he said. 'You will have to ring them. I don't know how much it costs but you have to do it straight away or they will close you down'.

'Ok what about the other things I need for the opening license'.

'You need to pass food handling exam which costs about 30 euros and also pass the inspection by the food department from the Town Hall. They will just turn up any time, so be ready. Here is a booklet of what they will be checking'.

'Ok thanks', I said. 'Anything else?'

'Yes, all your staff need the food handling certificate to work in the restaurant', said Carlos.

I thanked Carlos, left his office and immediately called the company at the top of his list.

Luckily they could speak English.

'I need a certificate, straight away...Dom Miguel, Calle Moncayo. When can you do it? Today would be great as we are closed, if possible.'

'Hang on', the chap replied.' Maybe we can'.

The guy came back to the phone.

'We can be there in two hours', he said. 'How much wood is there to treat?' he said.

'It's pretty much all wood, the bar, the walls the frontage, tables, chairs, everything apart from the floor and ceiling, I replied. 'How much will it be?'

'We can do it for 1,300 euros and you will have your official certificate', he replied.

I had no choice or time to negotiate. 'Ok, two hours, see you then', I said.

'You must clear the restaurant before they start, it is a bit messy', he replied.

I dashed back to the restaurant, desperately trying to ring Steve and Liam to give me a hand.

As expected no answer.

I spent the next two hours, stripping the table cloths and using them to cover everything that was not wood ..fridges, glass washing and coffee machines, the till etc.

Next I moved all of the plants scattered around the restaurant outside. I moved all glasses hanging above and behind the bar into the kitchen and finally moved all of the bottles of wine from the racks around the walls into the storeroom.

It was almost 1pm when a chap walked into the restaurant.

'Hola, I am Javier from Fuego Tratamiento, the guys come in 15 minutes. I am here to check it is OK to start'.

Javier started to walk up and down the restaurant. 'You need to cover lamps inside and outside', he said.

I quickly grabbed some of the tablecloths and covered them as best I could.

'Can I open tomorrow?' I asked.

'Should be OK but needs to dry out, leave the doors open as much as you can', said Javier.

He made a call to his chaps, 'Listo, ven ahora'...Come now', he said.

Ten minutes later the three chaps looking like something from the ghostbusters movie came wandering down the street carrying their huge spray guns. A smaller chap struggled behind wheeling a cart with around four large containers of liquid.

They nodded in my direction and moved behind the bar connecting their spray guns to the containers and strapping them to their backs.

'You go outside now', said Javier. 'Lots of spray'.

I moved to the door as two guys started to spray the bar and wall behind. They moved like lightning along the wooden walls and pillars spraying every crevice thoroughly.

I looked back into the restaurant which looked like a foggy day in the English countryside and a crowd had gathered outside the restaurant wondering what all the commotion was about.

Karen from the restaurant three doors away sauntered up to me.

'What's happening, have you had a fire? she enquired.

'No, it's part of getting an opening license, the Town Hall guys said I had to close if I did not get this done', I said. 'Have you had yours done?'

'No', said Karen, 'Didn't know you had to'.

'Think I must have upset the Town Hall guys the other day', I responded.

The guys finished spraying the inside and after about one hour moved to finish off the doors outside.

'Terminado, finished', one of the ghostbusters uttered and Javier moved towards the bar which was still wet from the spraying'.

He wrote out the certificate, signed it and passed it to me.

'1300 euros, por favor', said Javier.

I counted out the cash and handed it to Javier.

Javier counted the cash carefully and passed me the certificate.

'Gracias', he said as we shook hands.

'Thank god that's over', I said as one or two of the observers outside ventured into the restaurant including Karen.

All of the surfaces were covered in a sticky liquid and the tablecloths covering the bottles were sodden with the liquid. The mist slowly began to clear.

'I'll have to clean this place top to bottom, before we open tomorrow', I said to Karen.

'Good luck with that', she replied as she left the restaurant.

I spent the next five hours with bucketloads of bleach cleaning the entire place from top to bottom and washed hundreds of glasses which although had been moved to the kitchen were all covered in the sticky solution. I still had not managed to raise Steve or Liam to help me although I was happy to have the certificate in my hand.

Sat by the door having a drink at around 11pm after five hours of cleaning the place I saw Javier coming up the street with one of his sidekicks.

As he spoke he had obviously had a drink or two.

'Hola, you owe me 100 euros. When I counted the money you gave me there was only 1200 euros not 1300', he said.

'No', I replied you checked it in the restaurant when I handed it over.

'Only 1200 I checked at the office', he replied, 'You must pay me or give me the certificate back', said Javier.

I quickly looked behind me where the certificate was sitting on top of the bar.

'No chance', I said as I moved from my seat to pick it up.

Javier was starting now to become a little more aggressive and walked into the restaurant.

'No, you cheat me, I want the money', he continued.

'Piss off you look as if you have drunk it tonight', I said, 'Can you leave now I am closing?'

'My job is in trouble if I do not have the money', he pleaded, holding his hands together and looking as if he was praying to me moving his head and clasped hands up and down in front of me, with a pained expression on his face.

'Tough, you are not getting anything. Can you leave?' I said.

Finally he turned, shuffled outside and wandered down the street muttering to his mate.

The Summer is Coming

By the end of May Steve had just about made the 1,000 euro profit to pay the rent on Boxto. He had tried opening during the week without any success, however we were still confident that things would pick up during the summer when apparently thousands of Spanish headed to the 'cooler' coast for their holidays.

The restaurant was improving slightly hitting the breakeven 470 euro average most nights but there was always one or two nights when we struggled to pull in customers.

I paid the 2,000 euro rent all in cash of course to the Dom Miguel landlord, an old Spanish chap called Alberto who owned lots of properties and was making a fortune out of his rental income. I was also just about able to cover the staff wages, service costs and the apartment rental on time but was living right on the edge and could do without things like the money the Fire Certificate had cost me.

In early June I visited the bank to check the business account. I guessed that there should be about 2,000 euros in the account from the credit and debit card payments which amounted to about 20% of my nightly takings.

I requested a statement from the teller and the account showed me a negative balance of 50 euros.

'Where is my money from the credit card payments?' I asked feeling a bit worried.

'It's OK it takes thirty days to process ...they will be in the day after tomorrow', said the teller.

'Fine', I replied'. 'Thanks for your help', and left the bank feeling relieved.

Two days passed and I returned to the bank, going through the same procedure and still found my account in debit.

'You said two days', I said to the teller.

'Hang on', she replied, as she made her way to see her boss Christina.

I could see and hear the teller and Christina in the side office frantically looking through screens of information and making telephone calls.

After about ten minutes, Christina appeared.

'The credit card machine account was not changed for you', said Christina nervously.

'Why not?' I replied.

'Not sure, but definitely has not been changed', she said again.

'So where is the money?' I said, 'I have been using it for over a month now', I continued.

'In the old account', she said.

I was becoming angry now.

'For god's sake...the moneys going into George's account', I said, 'It's your mistake you should pay me the money'.

'No, no not possible', replied Christina, 'You will have to try and get money from George the previous owner'.

'Great', I replied, 'So when it be transferred to me?' I asked.

'Will take one hour', I promise you', replied Christina.' Ready to use tonight and your payments will be processed the next day'.

'Promise me and pigs might fly. Anyway she', pointing to the teller, 'said it takes thirty days to process each payment', I replied. 'Make sure it happens', as I left the bank feeling extremely annoyed.

'No, that is wrong payments are processed the next day, minus 2% commission', replied Christina. 'It takes one day not thirty'.

'Suggest you train your staff', I replied moving towards the door looking at the teller who was looking very uncomfortable.

I immediately rang George and left a desperate message explaining what had happened. To be honest I didn't really know if George was still in the country.

George did not return my call and I resigned myself to having lost 2,000 euros which was the last thing I needed.

That same evening in the restaurant, Rafael, George's helper appeared in the restaurant.
'Will have cheque for you tomorrow' said Rafael, 'Had a call from George I will get cheque tomorrow...2,100 euros and twenty for me of course'.

'Very happy with that', I replied and my mood lifted immediately.

Things are looking up I thought and the next day I had news that the house sale in the UK was going through the following week and my wife Barbara could submit her notice at work and join me in Spain in July.

In late June the hygiene inspector, a very smart young lady called Veronica from the Government food department arrived unannounced as I was cleaning the floor.

'Hola, always good to see cleaning', she said. 'Can I check a few things with you?'

'Ok no problem', as I led her into the kitchen where she opened the fridges to check that they all had temperature controls or thermometers inside.

The kitchen was fairly new anyway and had in built dials displaying the temperature, and it was always cleaned by Hamed and Halima at the end of every night. Veronica checked all of the kitchen equipment, chopping boards etc.

She moved behind the bar and checked the fire extinguishers and fridges under the bar which although a bit older had thermometers clipped to the inside of each one. She was impressed. The only failure, which I thought was typical, was the fridge I had dragged down from the 'Pig' last month.

'You need a thermometer here', she said. 'That is all'.

She then started to explore two small storerooms at the end of the restaurant where I kept some of the food, mainly cans, cartons, spaghetti, rice etc. Basically everything that did not need to be refrigerated. The food was all stacked up on top of each other on the floor.

'Oh dear', said Veronica, 'You must not keep food on the floor...cucarachas, cockroaches'.

'No problem', I replied, 'I will build some shelves'.

'Can I see your food handling certificate?' asked Veronica.

'Going on the course next week', I lied.

Veronica handed me a sheet of official looking paper and wrote in English the things I had to do before I could finally be given my food hygiene licence.

'Fine, not too much, I will be back in two or three weeks to check', she said, as she walked towards the door and out of the restaurant seeming to be quite happy.

Filling the restaurant was still proving to be a real challenge. As the weather was becoming a lot hotter now it was June, it was very easy to fill the terrace which had around six tables and could seat up to twenty customers, but it was impossible to drag them inside the restaurant with around fifty seats even though there were two large sets of doors opening onto the terrace. Customers wanted to people watch as they were eating and we were averaging about thirty covers a night which was around the breakeven point on the basis there were no surprise expenses.

The work itself during the evenings was good fun and I made lots of new friends who became returning customers even during their week's holiday and I also had a few locals coming back. It looked like we were on the right track but I figured it would take some time to fill the place, and after all it was not yet peak season.

I clearly remember one particular night at around 07.30pm when around a dozen customers arrived at the restaurant dressed in what I thought was fancy dress. There were around six young guys about sixteen years old dressed in yellow from top to bottom with flowing black capes and four or five young girls around the same age. An older guy obviously the boss was dressed the same except for a reddish coloured cape. The girls were dressed in black tops and long peach coloured skirts.

I jumped from behind the bar and with Everaldo began to pull four tables together so they could all sit together.

I welcomed the group and handed them the menus asking as usual if they wanted any drinks while they were deciding what to eat.

'We are a choir from Finland', the older guy said. 'We are singing at the Salon Varietes at 9 o'clock tonight'. The Salon Varietes was the only theatre in Fuengirola, quite small which regularly staged plays and musicals. We often had customers who were planning to go to this particular theatre as it was only around 200 metres from the restaurant.

During the meal the young guys kept wandering up to the bar to buy their drinks separately which was a little unusual.

'Just shout and I will come to the table', I said.

One of the young guys leaned across the bar and whispered. 'We will order orange juice or coke', he said,' Can you add vodka when we make the order? Don't let him see', as he nodded towards the older chap.

At the end of the main course the older guy beckoned me across.

'Can we sing?' he said.

Inside the restaurant there were only two other tables busy.

'Hang on', I said.

I walked over to the other customers to make sure they were OK with the impromptu entertainment.

I walked back to the chap and said. 'Yes they are OK, go for it'.

He stood up and counted the choir into their first song which was excellent. Even Hamed came out of the kitchen to listen. After each song the young guys in turn sauntered up to the bar to refill their drinks.

As agreed they ordered orange juice or coke.

Behind the bar, hidden from view I filled the glasses with ice and added a glug of vodka, and half filled the glass with the prerequisite orange juice or cola. They paid for each drink separately in cash and moved back to the table. This happened around three or four times in the next hour and with each drink the singing seemed to get a little louder.

At around 8pm they all left the restaurant much noisier and livelier than when they came in and I wished them luck for their performance. They had about half an hour to sober up.

On a different night which I still find a little weird a guy of around sixty came limping into the restaurant with a young dolly bird in her early thirties on his arm.

As normal I took the menu to the table and asked for drinks.

To my surprise the guy said, 'Do you know who I am?'

Looking closely I replied 'Sorry, I don't recognise you'.

The young lady looked embarrassed and said, 'Stop it, just order some drinks'.

'I'm Jim Mccalliog', he said, 'Have you heard of me?'

'Ah, yes' I replied, 'Played for Sheffield Wednesday didn't you?'

'And Chelsea and Manchester United and Scotland', he replied seeming to be quite upset that I hadn't mentioned these more famous clubs.

'Do you want my autograph for the bar?' he said.

Not really I thought to myself as I responded with 'Yes, that would be great'.

He signed a piece of paper with 'Best Wishes from Jim Mccalliog Chelsea and Manchester United' and handed me the paper. No mention of Sheffield Wednesday.

'What's your best wine?' he asked, obviously trying to impress his girlfriend.

I had no idea but pointed to the expensive wine on the menu, some of which I had never heard of.

'You will know better than me, I'm sure', I said as he selected a bottle of merlot dated 1997 at 40 euros.

He left the restaurant leaving a two euro tip on the table.

'What a prat', I said out loud to Everaldo as I threw his autograph in the bin.

I was now learning the business fast and as long as I kept to my schedule starting at 7am six days a week I began to feel more in control. Hamed let me use his car which was a huge help.

I regularly spoke to my sister Barbara who was fifty fifty owner of the Dom Miguel and my frustration with the numbers coming into the restaurant not surprisingly began to worry her.

One night at around 8pm, as I was sat in my usual anxious state after a full day's work waiting for customers the phone rang.

It was Barbara who was ringing for an update.

'We have got three bloody customers and it's 8' o'clock over here, I've had enough. This is pointless', I said.

We ended up having a huge row as obviously she had invested most of her savings in the restaurant but also in trusting me to look after her investment.

'Look', I finally said. We have three choices if you are not happy. Either we sell the place now, You buy me out or I will buy you out. Let me know what you want to do!!!'.

The phone rang later in the evening. It was my sister Barbara.

'Right I have spoken to Richie', her husband, 'We want either to sell it or you buy us out', she said.

'OK, I will buy you out then. You tell me what I owe you and I will see the abogado to draw up the new contract giving me full ownership'.

By early the following week I had sent my sister Barbara her money and she had signed the new contract stipulating that myself and my wife Barbara now owned the restaurant one hundred percent. It was totally our problem now to make or break the business with all of our cash invested in it.

One day towards the end of June I followed the normal routine for the big shop borrowing Hamed's car for the trip. Now as explained before, the nearest legal place to the restaurant to park the car was in a public car park around 400 metres away across the busy main coast road. It was not really practical to park there and make three or four trips with trolley loads of food to and from this car park.

There were a couple of places to park illegally much closer and I usually used a space close to my local cafe on the front. I always asked the staff in the cafe who I knew quite well by now to keep an eye out for the local plod while I ran with my trolley between the car and the restaurant.

On finishing, I always moved the car to a side street where there were sometimes a few spaces available around 200 metres from the restaurant. Hamed picked the car up after finishing his shift to drive back to his apartment.

This particular night just after exchanging the usual 'hasta manana' goodnight to Hamed and sitting down for my late meal Hamed returned unexpectedly.

'Where is the car?' he said

'Usual place', I replied

'No, no you show me', said Hamed.

I locked the restaurant and headed up the road with Hamed and the car was gone.

'Shit', I said, 'I know I locked it'.

'Should not park here..residents', said Hamed ' Reported to police'.

Hamed made a quick phone call to the local police station.

'Yes, it's there, in the car pound, cannot pick it up till the morning', said Hamed who was not very happy.

'Fine to pay police and fine to pay car pound', he continued.

The next day Hamed came into the restaurant as usual with two bills in his hand.

'You pay me now, 70 euros for police and 80 euros for pound', said Hamed

I duly handed over the cash and apologised again.

I decided that I needed to get my own transport as soon as possible and wasn't offered use of his car again.

What I did not know at this point was that this would be one of many trips to the police station and car pound.

During service that night Everaldo had heard about the problem with the car.

'I have a friend with a scooter for sale', he said. '650 euros and two helmets included'.

'I have never driven a scooter in my life', I replied.

'I teach you it's easy, if you let me borrow it now and again'.

'Ok, let me see it tomorrow', I said. '2 o'clock after the deliveries'.

I thought that a scooter would be ideal to speed up my shopping trips during the week even though I would still need to hire a car when I needed to do the Malaga run.

The next afternoon Everaldo appeared riding the scooter through the restaurant door.

I knew nothing about scooters, just that it looked OK.

'Let's go to the Feria', said Everaldo 'It's quiet there and I can teach you to ride it....jump on the back'.

Everaldo handed me a helmet and we sped off up to the Feria.

The Feria in Fuengirola is the area where the Spanish have their festivals, the main one is in July. More on that later.

We arrived at the Feria which was deserted and I sat on the bike ready for my first ever lesson.

Everaldo took me through the controls and after a rocky start soon I was able just about to manoeuvre the machine without falling off, but the thought of the benefits of having some transport overrode any fears I may have had.

'OK, I'll have it', I said to Everaldo, and we exchanged cash for the keys.

'Right off you go', said Everaldo, 'I need to see someone'.

'What, I cannot ride this back to the restaurant on my own'.

'You'll be fine', said Everaldo as he walked off laughing.

Less than thirty minutes after ever riding a scooter in my life I was in among the local traffic, heart in mouth heading back towards the coast. I made it without falling off which I was quite pleased about.

The next day I ventured out in trepidation on my scooter to do my daily shopping. I decided to go as far as Lidl which was about two miles away.

I finished my shopping and walked to the scooter with four full bags of food to take back. Standing in front of the bike I pondered ways of actually carrying the stuff safely, becoming more and more anxious.

I looked around for inspiration observing the local traffic which was around thirty per cent bikes and scooters. Some of the scooters passing by were loaded with bags, boxes, ladders, small fridges and even infants strapped to the back.

I carefully placed the four heavy bags of shopping between my feet and set off wobbling all over the road.

I had travelled around 50 metres and yes it happened. One of the bags was moving further and further to the right under my feet as I was driving along. Desperately trying to push it back into the middle of the scooter with my right foot one of the bags balanced on top of it spilled open. I was now trying to keep the bag from opening further with my knees when I lost control completely. I lurched over towards the pavement and just about managed to stop the bike from tipping over on top of me as I lost control.

The contents of the bags were scattered across the pavement which proved to be a great source of amusement to the passing traffic, pipping their horns in appreciation.

Slowly picking the bike up, and re bagging the shopping I set off again very slowly this time managing to reach the restaurant without killing myself or more importantly losing any of the food. Anyway, I had saved twenty minutes of my time which really was very important to me. Over the next few weeks I was racing around the town like a local managing to squeeze an extra 45 minutes of free time out of my usual 18 hour working day.

The trick I discovered was to use a very large cotton linen bag with two long straps at the top that are used to carry bedding and suchlike. Then to stuff all of the carrier bags full of groceries into this single larger bag. Then run the straps over the seat and sit on them. My record was seven bags and I could have managed more if my legs were a bit longer.

During the last week in June I was sat on the balcony in the apartment when Liam arose from his slumbers.

'My mum is not very well at home, I want to go back', he said.

'No problem, you need to go. Hope she is OK. I'll pay for your trip', I replied

'I want to go back for good', said Liam, 'I do not want to work at Botxo any more'.

I was a bit stunned by this as this was only Liam's second month in Fuengirola and I felt a little responsible for the situation as Liam had given up his job in the UK to be here to help Steve.

'Why don't you visit your mum and decide then what to do?' I suggested. 'What about working in the restaurant instead? I could definitely do with a hand during the day'.

Liam returned to the UK the next day to see his mum, and surprisingly appeared back at the apartment three days later.

'I'll work in the restaurant if the offer is still open', said Liam.

'OK great', I replied, thinking that I would have to replace Eva with Liam. Eva was working cash in hand and getting rid of Everaldo would be more complicated because of his contract.

'I'll have her in Boxto', piped up Steve who was listening to the conversation, and obviously saw Eva as a great asset to get the guys into his bar.

That evening at the end of the shift I explained the situation to Eva who I think was more pleased about the offer to work in Boxto rather than being sacked from the Dom Miguel. Talk about a lucky win, win.

For the next two weeks, every Monday when the Dom Miguel was closed, I made a point of myself Liam and Steve hiring a car and going out for the day or having an evening meal together.

One Monday morning we decided to travel down the coast to Gibraltar which was about one hour away. We parked up on the Spanish side of the Rock and walked through customs into Little Britain, across the airport runway and into the main town.

'Let's go up the rock', said Liam and we headed to the far end of the little town towards the chair lifts. Ascending the rock to the top like typical tourists we decided to walk back down via the paths which criss crossed up and down the rock back down to the road below. Liam started walking down the path ahead of me and Steve.

Half way down the path we heard a loud shout.

'Come here you little bastard. It's got my bloody bag', coming from Liam as we watched him chase a tiny little monkey up onto a small rock face carrying his plastic bag. Now watching Liam run is quite a funny sight at the best of times as he is a big lad, but watching him scrambling up the rock face chasing the monkey was something else.

Myself and Steve were cheering on Liam in tears of laughter, when suddenly the little monkey who was above Liam perched on a rock suddenly turned around, raised itself on two legs and screeched at him baring a huge set of teeth.

Liam stopped in his tracks exclaimed words to the effect of 'fuck me' and he crashed back down the path running away from this little monkey as fast as his legs would carry him. Steve and I were now in absolute hysterics rolling around on the ground to the point where it began to hurt our ribs.

Liam did not seem to be so impressed. 'Very funny', he said.

'What was in the bag?' said Steve.

'Just some water and a picnic', he replied.

'Maybe you've pulled and the monkey just wanted a meal with you', said Steve

The response sent us into another spasm of uncontrolled laughter. Again Liam was not amused.

On the Monday evenings the three of us would sometimes wander down to the grotty port area for a meal but more importantly for me to pay a visit to see Eddie, the guy recommended by big Ron from 'The Pig', to stock up on my 6 euro per bottle spirits to sell in the restaurant.

It always depressed me going down the port and made me thankful that I did not buy a business there. In one of the many quiet restaurants in the port we met a couple from Durham called Bill and Sue who owned a very small restaurant and had been open for around five months .

We got chatting with the usual question. 'How's business?' I asked Bill.

Now the standard answer from any bar owner when asked this question by a stranger is always 'Not too bad'.

'Got a restaurant in Fish Alley', I replied. 'Business is not great up there', I said.

Bill replied, 'To be honest it's crap here, I made 45 euros last night and 65 the night before'.

I said to myself that if that was me I would top myself and to stop worrying so much about everything as it could be a lot worse. At least I was just about breaking even.

I felt really sorry for Bill and to be honest all of the many other bar owners in the port and we made a point of eating at his restaurant every Monday. It was one of the saddest things which will stick in my mind forever seeing his empty cafe each Monday with one table with a reserved plaque stuck in the middle waiting for us to arrive.

Bill also had a transit van parked in the port carpark and he agreed to loan it to me to do the big shop for 20 euros plus petrol which was a great help to me and for him probably matched half his daily income.

In the Dom Miguel Liam started working with Everaldo who was not too happy about Eva having to leave.

Over the coming nights Everaldo and Liam were locking horns around three times a night and obviously did not get on. It was actually like running two restaurants consisting of Everaldo's tables and Liam's. The atmosphere deteriorated and Hamed was becoming quite angry when the plates ready for a particular table had to wait for either Liam or Everaldo to appear as they refused to take the food to a table that was not theirs. Something had to give.

'This isn't working, is it', I said to Liam at the end of the shift.

'No', said Liam, 'I cannot work with him'.

'I can see that', I replied, 'But I cannot get rid of Everaldo. He is on a contract till the end of July'.

'To be honest', Liam replied, 'I still want to go back to look after my mum'.

The next day Liam left Fuengirola for good.

It was however not too difficult recruiting waiting staff for the restaurants in Fuengirola. Now chefs that is a completely different story which I'll explain shortly.

Mikey the DJ working in Boxto had a girlfriend called Vicky who met him on holiday and decided to join him in Fuengirola two weeks later. Vicky was a singer with a bubbly personality and sense of humour very similar to Marti Caine and was looking for work in the bars around Fuengirola. Anyway, she had a half sister called Katy who was also looking for work who lived in Fuengirola with her father who operated one of the many estate agents. Katy was tall, blonde and very confident and certainly could charm customers, especially the guys into the restaurant. Perfect for the restaurant, Spanish speaking and she was ready to start immediately. She was the fourth waiter I had employed since the restaurant opened in May, two months ago.

Steve had no problem with Liam leaving as he was now very close to Mikey and Vicky who seemed to be at Boxto day and night just sat by the decks in the corner playing music.

The main problem was Steve's reluctance to keep the place clean. More and more of my time was now spent during the afternoon at Boxto cleaning up, which wasn't too bad during the week as he had very few customers. On Friday and Saturday nights, however, mountains of rubbish needed to be cleared.

I really did not have any spare time to look after Boxto to clean the place and mentioned to Hamed that I needed some help for Steve.

'Wait', he said and started a conversation in Arabic with Halima, his kitchen assistant.

'Halima will clean for you on Saturday and Sunday mornings', said Hamed.

'Are you sure?' I replied, 'The place will be an absolute tip'.

For six euros an hour it was the best investment I made. I visited Boxto as part of my regular Saturday and Sunday routine to see if there was any money in the cigarette machine cash box and Halima, her brother and sister were all busy cleaning away in the bar.

Three people, working out at two euros an hour each. Perfect.

Boxto was however still not covering its costs, especially to pay the rent at the end of the month and I was quite concerned.

One day however completely out of the blue Steve arrived at the apartment and handed me 1,000 euros with a smug look on his face.

'There you go, rent for next month', he said, 'Brilliant aren't I'.

'Where the hell have you been hiding this?' I said.

Apparently, Danny, the coloured guy who worked in Boxto, the guy who rescued me from the local hookers a couple of months ago had a 'friend' who needed somewhere to have a party.

This friend of his came to see Steve and offered 1,000 euros to book the whole bar for the night. Steve just had to provide the bar staff and he would supply his own booze.

Steve accepted the offer after speaking to Danny who suggested he did not ask any questions about his friend's employment history. I was pleased, Boxto had made a profit in June.

Danny was a really nice guy, however I found out he was an illegal immigrant who was constantly on the lookout for the local police.

One Saturday morning I arrived early at Boxto for my usual inspection.

Danny came running into the bar.

'Phil, do not leave the door open, it is not safe. Always lock the door', he said.

I noticed on the pavement outside two scruffy looking guys, obviously still half pissed looking across into the bar.

'They have knives', said Danny pointing to the two guys in the street. 'Always lock the door when you are alone', he repeated.

Danny moved back to the door and shouted at the two guys outside in Spanish and they scuttled off down the road.

I had spoken to Danny only three times now and he had saved me from trouble twice. I never left the door unlocked again when I was alone in Boxto.

During the final week in June I had to go back to the UK for two days to help the wife move house and left Steve in charge of the restaurant.

He worked with me for a couple of days, learning the till and how to generally get the place up and running. The day before I left I did a mega shop to make sure he had everything for the time I was away. We agreed that Vicky, Mikey's girlfriend, would also help Katy and Everaldo in the restaurant, while I was away.

I headed for the UK and spent the next two days, with the help of my son David and wife Barbara moving from a huge five bed roomed house to a very small three bed semi, luckily with an attached garage.

We made around ten trips between houses using a large transit van owned by my son's friend Steve. The amount of stuff I had accumulated would not fit the tiny property which was completely full even after the third trip in the van.

After many attempts we managed to find a home for everything. The garage was absolutely full to the rafters with chairs stacked on top of sofas, with boxes sitting on top of the chairs. The loft in the house as well was completely stuffed with everything ranging from beds to suitcases and boxes full of books, clothes and other assorted bits and pieces.

Finally it was all done, after another 18 hour day this time back in the UK and now Barbara, my wife could join me out in Spain in the July once she had worked her notice period.

July - The Spanish are coming

I returned to Fuengirola on the 2nd of July after doing my duty moving house at about 1pm to find as expected Steve still asleep in the apartment and went straight to the restaurant to make sure it was still in one piece.

The till was empty except for a shopping list from Hamed sitting on top of the till. Obviously Steve must have expected the restaurant fairies to do this shopping ready for the night's service.

I jumped on my scooter with my trusty cotton laundry bag stuffed under the seat and set off for my usual supplies from Lidl and Mercadona.

I returned quickly to the restaurant and started the daily cleaning routine, which seemed no surprise to have been neglected over the past two days. Maybe Steve thinks there are cleaning fairies as well, I thought to myself.

I went back to the apartment at around 4pm for a quick change and shower and more importantly any news from Steve, as I could guarantee that he would have some stories to tell.

I sat with Steve on the balcony waiting for his briefing.

'You'll never guess', said Steve.

'Oh god what's happened', I said.

'The American guy went mental last night in the restaurant', Steve continued.

The American guy who I have not mentioned lived in the apartment block next door to the restaurant. What he was doing in

Fuengirola I will never know but he was obviously living by himself and seemed to be slightly out of it most of the time.

Most early afternoons just as we opened he would come into the restaurant, order a coffee or a bowl of soup and sit at the bar and talk mostly bollox about the American forces. In a short time we learnt that he would agree with any old rubbish that you could make up such as the well known story about the Japanese invading Britain, and myself and Steve often amused ourselves inventing rubbish which he always agreed was kosher and he already knew about.

He said he had been in the U.S. military and had come to Fuengirola for a long holiday.

Steve also had had a bit of fun during the last month when he served him his coffee, but rather than giving him a sachet of sugar on his saucer he provided a sachet of brown sauce.

Without a flicker on his face he opened the sachet of sauce tipped it into the coffee and began to drink the concoction. I actually think he quite enjoyed the coffee and it amused myself and Steve watching from behind the bar. Maybe we had invented a new drink to sell.

'Anyway', Steve continued.

'We were quite busy' he said, 'and the American guy started shouting .... They're coming!!, they're coming!!', waving his arms around and then he grabbed hold of one of the customers and pulled him out of his chair. I thought he was going to beat him up'.

'Shit, what did you do', I said.

'I grabbed him from the back, held his arms behind him and threw him out of the door'. said Steve.

'What happened then?' I enquired.

'Nothing' he just walked back to his apartment as if nothing had happened. High as a bloody kite', said Steve.

That night the American chap walked casually into the restaurant as usual

'You can't come in here', I said and stopped him as he approached the bar.

'Why, what's up?' he drawled in his American accent.

'You can't go frightening my customers', I said calmly, 'You are barred'.

He looked quite hurt as he turned saying, 'I don't understand you Brits'.

He left the restaurant with absolutely no recollection of what had happened the night before and actually I never saw him again.

I returned to the Dom Miguel that evening just as Hamed was coming down the road.
He walked as usual to the store cupboard to connect up the gas ready to switch on the ovens.

'No gas', said Hamed. 'I told Steve to get some'.

'Shit', I thought.

'Go and see Indians across the street', said Hamed.

I dashed across the street towards the Indian restaurant and begged the waiter for a bottle of gas.

'One', the Indian waiter said, 'You can have one'.

'Cheers', I replied as I gave him 20 euros and dragged the bottle back across the street.

'We need three', said Hamed.

'Shit I replied, 'Would two last the evening'.

'Maybe, but can't promise', said Hamed.

I had no other choice now so I dragged my trusty shopping trolley out of the storeroom and wandered up and down the street looking for spare bottles from other restaurants much to the amusement of all of the waiters standing up and down the road.

Eventually I managed to beg another two bottles and we were up and running again. Steve must think there are gas fairies as well I said to myself.

That same evening I had a visitor to the restaurant who I took a while to recognise. It was Rafael, now out of work since George had now left Spain. He had morphed into a drunken tramp in a few short weeks.

I had one or two customers in the restaurant at the time as he walked unsteadily up to the bar.

'Please help me', pleaded Rafael 'Lend me 50 euros. I will pay you back tomorrow...I promise... I need to pay rent'.

'No', I replied, 'I cannot afford it at the moment'.

Hamed was watching from the kitchen.

Rafael was speaking quite loudly and customers were now looking across at the scene.

He started to become a little louder with his pleading and I was feeling more and more uncomfortable.

He then dropped to his knees, clasped his hands together moving them up and down in front of me as if praying and with a pained expression continued his pleading.

'Tomorrow, will pay you back tomorrow', he pleaded.

I needed to get him out of the restaurant as quickly as possible so I handed him a 50 euro note.

'Gracias, gracias', said Rafael as he picked himself up from the floor.

'Ok, see you tomorrow', I replied. Hamed stood shaking his head.

I did see him the next day, but this time he came to the restaurant at around 11pm carrying a frozen pizza.

'Where is the 50 euros?' I enquired.

'Manana', he said, 'You will have it tomorrow'.

'Will you cook this for me?' said Rafael.

'Ok, but only this one time', I replied.

Hamed was again shaking his head as I handed him the pizza to cook in the microwave.

'Manana, I will have your money tomorrow...no problem', he said as he walked out of the door, pizza in hand.

The following night I did not see Rafael at all, however, around four of his new found friends who were also alcoholic tramps appeared in the bar carrying a range of frozen foods begging me to cook it for them. Again I had a few customers in the restaurant.

This time I had had enough.

'Get out now or I will call the police. Get out now !!!', I shouted at the four of them.

I think the loudness and tone of my voice surprised them as they all quickly scuttled out of the restaurant.

I never did see Rafael or my 50 euros again.

To continue this theme of me being the local money lending service, Katy my waitress asked for a couple of days off as she had some relatives coming over to visit.

Everaldo offered to cover her for the two nights with his mate Manuel who was an experienced waiter who worked in a tapas bar up the road.

Manuel was a young Spanish chap and obviously had some relationship with Everaldo who apparently swung both ways and the two of them were in their element prancing up and down the restaurant shouting orders to each other looking as if they were on some mission to impress me and each other as to how good they were at the job.

At the end of the second evening I was at the till counting out the wages for Manuel for his two nights work.

'Can you lend me 50 euros for my rent?' he started to plead, 'Please, please will pay you back on Friday'.

'No chance', I said, 'I don't even know you'.

He then transformed himself into the stereotypical Spanish pose of clasping his hands together, praying to me with that pained expression on his face.

This was now the third time in a few weeks that this was happening in front of me and after the earlier episodes with Javier from the Fire Certification company and Rafael and I could feel the anger fill my body from my feet through my legs and stomach up to my head. I was consumed with rage and let fly.

'What the fuck are you praying to me for?' I shouted at Manuel imitating his actions.

'What's your bloody problem? I continued angrily. 'Stop it now and get your stupid arse out of here and don't come back. And no you are not getting 50 euros. Piss off now or I will come round there and throw you out myself'.

Hamed and Everaldo looked at me in complete astonishment as Manuel with a look of horror on his face quickly left the restaurant.

Even today when I see Spanish footballers 'praying' to referees in this manner it makes my blood boil.

During the first week in July I had booked the final piece in the jigsaw to obtain my restaurant license. The food handling hygiene certificate course at an office on the outskirts of the town.

On the day of the course I walked into the classroom to be greeted by the teacher and around twenty other candidates. The course was totally in Spanish and I just about figured out that the exam at the end would be multiple choice.

Now, my Spanish is not great except for being able to just about take food orders at the restaurant, but when the core of the course is about different types of infections and bacteria that is another story.

I sat for three hours solid listening to a myriad of words which had no meaning to me at all.

When the painful session finally ended the teacher handed out an examination paper with fifteen multiple choice questions. The pass mark I think she said was thirteen correct answers. I sat and tried to translate what was in front of me but could not understand any of the questions let alone attempt the answers.

Looking around the room the other candidates were all busy filling in the answers so I thought to myself that guessing was the only option I had.

I randomly filled in the answers and walked to the front of the class where a young guy was marking the papers and another chap beside him taking the fees for the course.

I stood in a line waiting for my turn, trying to peek at other candidate's papers without any success.

Soon it was my turn and the guy quickly marked my paper.

'Ocho correcto...eight correct', he said.

'I don't know Spanish', I replied, 'I basically just guessed the answers randomly'.

'Ok', the young chap replied, 'Go and pay now', as he pointed to the chap a few feet away taking the 30 euros.

Disappointed I handed over my cash ready to leave and to my surprise he handed me a 'Certificado de Pase' with my name typed at the bottom.

'Have I passed?' I said.

'Si,si...you pass no problem', he replied.

I walked out feeling absolutely thrilled and thought to myself that I must try for many more qualifications over in Spain.

The next day I proudly went off to see Carlos with my newly acquired Fire Certificate, Hygiene Certificate and the Restaurant inspection paper from Veronica.

'Perfecto', said Carlos, 'We can now get the new opening license. Remember to sort out shelves and thermometer for the freezer as soon as possible, but we can now get the license'.

'By the way come in tomorrow with your papers and invoices your accounts are due', said Carlos.

The next day I dropped most but not all of my invoices, all dutifully stamped with my NIE number with Carlos to do my first quarter accounts.

He rang me later that evening.

'12 euros tax', said Carlos.

'Is that it?' I replied.

'Yes', he replied. 'You have a very good accountant'.

'12 euros you have to be kidding', I thought to myself feeling very pleased with the outcome.

Two days later the opening license certificate was posted to the restaurant. I was now trading legally for the first time.

As I said previously I was becoming an expert scooter rider and continued to fly around Fuengirola doing my daily shop. It was Monday, my day off and I decided to put up the shelves in the two storerooms ready for my next inspection from Veronica.

I carefully measured up and headed for a large hardware store which was next to the Lidl supermarket about one mile from the restaurant.

I soon found the shelving I needed, about seven shelves 2 metres by ½ metre lengths together with some fittings.

I carried them over my shoulder back to the scooter and it struck me that this load was different to my normal shopping load, especially the 2 metre lengths of shelving.

I sat on the scooter with the shelving across my knees and set off slowly.

Ahead was a busy junction with three lanes and I needed to pass down the inside lane. The other two lanes were busy.

I headed for my lane and realised that my two metre lengths would not fit the gap ahead and had to swerve off the road onto the central reservation.

This also made me realise that there was no way I would be able to drive up the narrow side streets leading to the restaurant further down the road.

There was only one thing for it, I would have to leave the bike and carry the shelves to the restaurant.

It was a very hot day about 85 degrees as I set off with the seven shelves loaded on my right shoulder leaving the scooter on the central reservation.

After less than 100 metres my shoulder and back were racked with pain due to the heavy weight I was trying to carry.

'Shit, I can't do this', I thought. 'This will finish me off'.

I set off again, this time stopping after 50 metres. I still had about 700 metres to go.

For the next two hours and a dozen stops I eventually reached the restaurant. My whole body was broken and I was completely dehydrated as I lay slumped on a stool leaning on the bar drinking lots of water. The shelves didn't get fixed that day. God I need a car I thought to myself.

July is the time that the Spanish take their holidays. They all migrate from the inland towns, Seville, Granada, Cordoba to the coast where it is considered to be much cooler and we were expecting the restaurant and more particularly Boxto to be busy.

The Spanish tend to go to the beach around 4pm and stay there until it starts to become dark and then they hit the restaurants around 9 or 10 at night. July was a painful month in terms of business in the restaurant.

I was still managing to fill the terrace but as it became hotter and hotter no-one wanted to eat early apart from a few Brits, or more importantly sit inside the restaurant. I needed to do something quickly to fill up the 50 potential covers inside.

I decided to offer free wine before 8pm to attract more early evening customers. This had some effect particularly from the Brits who even though were given some free wine always without exception ordered extra drinks on top. I think the British mentality is different from the Spanish as the few Spanish that did arrive early took full advantage of this offer…'vino gratis'..free wine. They thought it was Christmas come early.

You can easily identify the Brits abroad. At least one in every party you notice have been on the beach in the sun just a little too long given away by bright red faces and painful looking arms and legs. All they wanted was to sit in the cool shade and drink.

Looking to take advantage of this, I decided to advertise aggressively that we had air conditioning inside the restaurant, even though this meant closing the two large double doors opening on to the terrace area and pissing off Everaldo and Katy, the waiters, who had to open and close them to reach the terrace with the food.

This approach helped to pull some extra customers into the restaurant who were relieved to be out of the sun and being cooled down at the same time.

There is a saying in Spain. 'The Spanish need a waiter for every table', and I found out quickly that this was the case.

One particular night, quite early, with a few tables inside occupied by some Brits with young kids, six or seven Spanish pensioners wandered into the restaurant up to be bar.

I did my best after a struggle to understand them to serve them their drinks with a little help from Hamed who was watching through the kitchen hatch. They were all stood by the bar when one of the old chaps shouted across to me 'Comida,comida' …'food…food'.

'Ok', I replied and gathered up six menus and handed them one each.

Hamed was stood laughing by the kitchen.

'Phil, no, they want free food', he said.

'Free food', I replied astonished. 'They can bloody well pay for it like everyone else'.

The old people were all looking towards us holding the unopened menus muttering amongst themselves.

Hamed replied, 'I'll give them some olives', and proceeded to fill three small bowls.

Feeling quite uncomfortable by now I placed the olives on the bar and took back their menus.

'Gracias', one of the old ladies said.

They continued to finish their drinks and eat the olives, when out of the corner of my eye I spotted one of the older chaps spitting the large olive seeds out on to the floor.

To my astonishment this heralded a frenzy of olive seeds being spat all around the floor from both the old men and women alike.

Hamed could see the look on my face and was now creased up laughing behind the kitchen door.

I quickly ran around the front of the bar with two plastic buckets pointing at them sternly and mimicking to them as best I could to spit the seeds into the buckets and not onto the bloody floor. I don't think they understood my geordie accent.

Meanwhile the few Brits in the restaurant who were watching all of this going on were all in hysterics laughing.

Eventually, thank god they left with the Brits all thanking me for the best entertainment they had had in months. Anyway they all left good tips for their impromptu comedy show.

Meanwhile, there were nights in July when I did not have a single customer before 9pm and to sit paying four staff from 5pm was becoming really stressful.

However at 9pm all hell broke loose as customers all arrived at once between 9 and 10 and even later all wanting to sit on the terrace. The takings reflected this and although increasing slightly I was still just hitting the 500 to 550 euro per night figure.

At this point I made some slight adjustments, employing just one waiter Everaldo from 5pm with Katy arriving at 0730. I also asked Hamed and Halima to work an extra hour to finish at 1am rather than 12 which they agreed to do. I also employed one of Steve's PR mates, a young Irish guy called Shaun for two hours to stand outside the restaurant tempting customers to come in. Shaun spent most of his time chatting up passing young girls so the benefit of this move was very questionable.

Back to the earlier comment of the Spanish needing a waiter for every table. I found this to be very true although for some reason Everaldo loved the Spanish. Hamed was less impressed however.

A typical Spanish family scenario went as follows assuming four adults and two young kids.

Starter......bread....lots of bread....4 euros maximum and some house wine and water. The six of them would sit for one hour dipping their bread into olive oil as a starter. Now obviously olive oil is cheaper in Spain than the UK but is still quite expensive even in

Spain at around seven euros a bottle and they could easily go through a full bottle of the stuff.

Next two large salads between the six of them with more bread and olive oil...another hour gone and the noise levels keep increasing by about ten decibels after every glass of cheap wine. You can at this point notice other customers looking annoyed at the racket and shaking their heads in disapproval.

At this point the Spanish have completely forgotten about their kids who now bored stiff start running around the restaurant knocking over glasses and generally shouting at each other.

I now start to become annoyed and discreetly begin to follow the kids saying quietly, 'Sentarse, silencio'...'sit down, be quiet'.

The kids then look at you as if you are from Mars pretending that they don't understand.

'No entiendo', the kids' reply laughing...'don't understand'.

Meanwhile the parents are completely oblivious to all of this and their noise levels continue to rise. Next the parents want to order something slightly different than what are the main menu choices obviously, normally ending up with four or five large portions of a la carte starters with another mega salad and obviously more bread and olive oil. They then sit for another two hours until around 1230am randomly waving across for other bits and pieces, with the bored kids still running around.

At the end of their meal the table is a complete mess and I start to close the restaurant around them, switching off the music, stacking chairs on tables and changing tablecloths. This has no impression on them whatsoever.

Finally the bill, for the six of them it's around 80 euros. Eventually they leave with a tip ranging between 10 and 20 cents.

At the end of the evening Hamed comes across and says, 'Now you understand. A waiter for every table'.

'Now I understand', I replied.

To be fair to the Spanish I found that the above scenario only seemed to apply to those from the Costa del Sol region. I always found customers from the likes of Madrid, Bilbao and other regions to be very respectful although the tips they left at the end of the night were always dire.

The above scenario was repeated many times to the point where my heart sank slightly when they appeared and I certainly did not put as much effort pulling them in as I did when I started in the restaurant. The only real benefit for me was that they made the restaurant look busy even just one table of them based on the noise that they created.

Another problem I had with the Spanish during this time was that some of the younger lads didn't really want to pay. A couple of times they would sit on the terrace drinking a couple of bottles of San Miguel and just up and leave.

On one occasion I had two Spanish lads stood at the bar drinking each with a bottle of San Miguel. When they had finished they put two euros on the bar and turned to leave.

'That is cinco (5) euros', I shouted after them. Completely oblivious they just continued to wander out of the restaurant with me shouting after them.

From that day on I always asked for the money from the Spanish drinkers before I handed them the beer much to their annoyance. I never ever had to do this with any other nationalities.

As I spent more of my free time with other English bar owners what had happened to me was very common. It was clear that the Spanish, mainly those who lived on the Costa del Sol were not really keen on the English. To be honest at this point the feelings were becoming mutual.

I remember the 70's, when Spain started to become popular with the Brits. The Spanish then were fantastic in trying to make you welcome, the service was excellent although the food was inedible. Tourism made a lot of Spanish very rich and on joining the EU as the poorest country by far at the time they received mountains of cash to build the roads and infrastructure which Britain contributed a huge slice of. As the country particularly the tourist sector grew and Brits started to buy property and open businesses in Spain their attitude started to change towards the Brits and I have it on good authority from a Spanish chap who will be introduced later in this story, they are quite anti British.

An often repeated comment from big Ron and Dave was that the Spanish would still be digging potatoes if it were not for the British and they should remember that.

On the other hand Brits abroad have a reputation for being drunk and disorderly but in my experience they and other Northern Europeans and especially the Irish are saints.

I had a few nights when large groups of young guys from the UK came to the restaurant obviously after a few drinks. Ok, one or two were always a little worse for wear and became more and more boisterous as the night wore on, but all I had to do was have a quiet word to one of the guys who tended to be in charge of the group and the problem was sorted immediately.

Merry or sober the Brits, Irish and other Northern Europeans to a lesser extent treated you, your staff and the restaurant with respect. The older Brits really do never complain. I have even served the wrong food and they offered to eat that instead of what they had ordered as they didn't want to see food thrown away. They always pay the bill and start apologising to you if they have any sort of query or issue and always give good tips, especially the groups of young guys or girls.

It made me start to wonder why I would want to move away from the UK to live here.

One day in early July as I was heading for my scooter to do the usual quick shop, sitting on the seat I noticed that the front of the scooter with the handlebars parallel in front of me the front wheel was pointing distinctly to the right and not straight ahead. I started to move forward but it was obvious that something was wrong as I kept steering towards the kerb. Soon I gave up and set off of foot to do the shopping.

Later that day in the apartment I had a conversation with Steve. 'What's happened to the bike?' I asked Steve.

'Oh sorry dad, forgot to mention it. Had a slight accident yesterday', said Steve, 'The front wheel mounting needs realigning, I will sort it out', he continued. He never did of course.

Mentioning the problem to Hamed that night, the next day at lunchtime he appeared at the door as I was humping the empty gas bottles into the trolley ready to exchange them.

'Phil, come with me, got a car for you', said Hamed, '800 euros'.

'Ok', I replied, as Hamed made a quick call on his mobile.

After ten minutes a young Spanish guy, called Jose appeared at the door.

'Ready for a test drive', said Jose, 'Follow me'.

Myself and Hamed followed the guy to the car parked on the front and we all got into a fairly old Renault Meganne.

I set off driving along the front for about ten minutes and noticed that the clutch pedal was very, very stiff although it seemed to drive OK.

We soon parked up back where we started and the young Spanish guy said.

'Bueno, good car, yes'.

'The clutch is very stiff', I replied and Hamed translated this back to Jose.

'Si, si', Jose replied, 'Muy nuevo...very new'.

'He says it was changed last week and that is why it is stiff', said Hamed.

OK, I thought to myself it's worth a risk for 800 euros and as I do not have the scooter anymore, I need something.

Jose passed me the keys waiting for his 800 euros.

My instinct at this stage was not to trust anyone by default.

'I need to speak to my gestor, Carlos, before I hand over any money', I said to the young chap which Hamed duly translated.

I immediately rang Carlos to make an appointment for the next day.

'Meet me at Británico Associates at 10am tomorrow', I said to Jose and handed him back the keys.

The next day I met with Jose at 10am as agreed.

We walked into the office to be greeted by Carlos who positioned two chairs in front of his desk and started to speak in Spanish to Jose.

I did not understand the conversation but noticed that their voices were becoming a little louder as the conversation progressed.

Suddenly Jose stood up and walked to the door to leave muttering what I assumed to be some local expletives.

'Phil', said Carlos, 'Good job you came, it is not his car. He has no Libro de Registro del Coche...car registration document. He must have just got hold of the keys somehow'.

'Shit', I thought to myself and thanked Carlos.

'Always check with me', said Carlos, 'Never sign for anything unless I see it'.

'Ok, thanks again', I replied as we shook hands and I left the office.

This episode had a huge affect on me and I made a very strong mental note not to trust anyone from now on in...except for Carlos. My personality was beginning to change now, and I knew I needed to become tougher to survive over here. Basically, everyone seemed to be on the take.

That evening I rang Barbara, my wife who was due to join me for good in Spain and we agreed that she would arrange to transport my car across from the UK. I had to have transport now the scooter was off the road and I couldn't trust anyone over here to buy one from.

After the lucky break in June of the 1,000 euros for Boxto, July was proving to be more of a struggle. Emero, the bouncer had now left Boxto to work for the nightclub next door and we had to hire a bouncer from a local British run agency.

This was not proving to be a success as the door takings through issuing the entry tickets were now running at less than 200 euros for Friday and Saturday evenings which were really the only two busy nights. The turnover of staff, both PR's and behind the bar seemed to change on a nightly basis and we were heading for a real shortfall on paying the rent at the end of the month.

I sat down with Steve and Mikey the DJ to find out what we could do to improve things.

'It's too hot in Boxto', they both said as one. 'The air conditioning is broken'.

'How much is that?' I replied.

'1200 euros, fully fitted', said Mikey. 'I know a Spanish firm who could do it straight away ready for Friday'.

'Ok, let's do it', I replied, 'We really have no choice. Get the guy to meet me here tomorrow at 11am to sort out the details'.

The next day the chap arrived who could speak very good English.

We shook hands. '1,200 euros fully fitted', I said.

'Yes, the chap replied, 'We can fit it above the door on the outside. You will not see it from the inside'.

'Sounds good. When can you start?'

'Manana, at 9', he replied.

'Can you be here for 9?' I said to Steve knowing that Steve had never seen 9am for three months.

'Guess, I'll have to be', said Steve.

The next day at around 10.30am Steve came walking quickly into the restaurant.

'The guy wants an extra 200 euros to stick the unit outside. He says he can only do it for 1,200 if we mount it inside'.

By now like I said my perceptions of the Spanish way of doing business was changing which was beginning to have a big affect on my attitude towards them.

'Go back and tell him to piss off. He agreed to do it for 1200 euros fitting the unit on the outside. If he now says it can't be done we will go somewhere else'.

Steve left the restaurant and returned at around 1pm.

'All done', he said.

'What for 1200 euros?' I asked

'Yes', said Steve.

'Fitted on the outside?' I enquired.

'Yes, fitted on the outside', he replied back smiling.

'Why do these guys always seem to try it on?' I said.

I was really now beginning to start to dislike the Spanish ways of doing business and becoming very distrustful of them all by this stage, with the exception of Carlos, my gestor.

Tomorrow the 17th July was the day when Barbara my wife was joining me for good with my car due to arrive on the 20th. My son David his friends Carl and Sam from the local village pub and one of Steve's friends Mark were also coming out for a week's holiday, all dossing down at the apartment as best they could.

I met them all the next day with Steve at the local Fuengirola train station and we all walked back through the town to the apartment. That night they all turned up at the restaurant for a quick meal ready for their night in Boxto with Steve. Barbara was helping me in the restaurant.

The car was not due to arrive for a couple of days and with the scooter out of action I took advantage of having two strapping young lads, David and Carl, to help me with the shopping.

One day we walked the mile or so from the apartment to Lidl where I really needed to stock up for at least two nights ahead.

As usual I quickly charged around Lidl with a trolley followed by the two lads pushing a backup trolley and loaded the two trolleys of shopping into twelve carrier bags, four each.

We set off back to the apartment carrying the bags. It was quite a hot day.

After around 200 metres the two lads began to show signs of discomfort and Carl put down the bags and sat down looking quite exhausted.

'What's up?' I asked Carl.

'I am knackered, I need a drink', said Carl.

'Ok', wait there', I replied and walked across the road to buy two cans of coke.

The two lads slowly drank the coke and with miserable expressions on their faces we set off again. After another 200 metres or so Carl and Dave were falling further and further behind me and had stopped again.

'Do you want to swap my bags for yours?' I said to Carl, 'Mine must be lighter'.

I exchanged the bags with Carl and we set off again.

After about 50 metres Carl piped up.' Can we swop back the bags?'

We had now just about reached the coast road back to the apartment and were on the final 500m metre stretch.

'Look, I have to go ahead, I've got things to do. I will see you at the restaurant', I said to the lads.

'OK, no problem', they both replied probably pleased to see the back of me. They looked quite ill with the heat and the weight of the bags at this point and were ready to drop.

I wandered ahead of them to the restaurant to drop off my bags.

Carl and David didn't arrive at the restaurant as promised.

I was a little worried and walked back to the apartment to find the two lads collapsed on the sofa with the eight bags of shopping in front of them. Carl was a complete mess.

I started laughing. 'Looks like I'll have to take this myself', I said

'We can manage two each', said David.

'Come on, let's just leave Carl to recover', I replied as myself and David picked up four bags each and walked again to the restaurant. We just left Carl on the settee. He looked traumatised.

For the rest of the their holiday the two lads seemed to keep themselves at a distance from me..not sure why.

'I bloody need that car,' I thought to myself.

Boxto continued to really struggle to make any money whatsoever now and I was becoming worried. There was little or no money to contribute to the rent let alone the service costs.

I regularly checked the state of Boxto every other afternoon and was spending more and more time having to clean the place.

I discussed this with Steve and Barbara basically telling him to get his finger out as I didn't have time to do this and as usual most conversations with Steve tended to escalate into a shouting match.

'Look if you can't run the bloody bar, I'll find someone else who can', I said, which ended the conversation with Steve close to tears and walking away with Barbara closely following her precious son as usual.

'Don't speak to him like that', said Barbara, 'You've really upset him now'.

'Upset him, I'll kill him', I replied as they both scuttled off together heading down the side street towards the coast.

It was a Monday evening and by 8pm neither of them had returned to the apartment.

I decided to try and find them and started to walk along Fish Alley and then down to the port area. Eventually I found them both sat in one of the bars and as soon as they spotted me off they ran off again.

The next day as usual with Steve and his friends still in bed I finished my daily chores for the restaurant and headed off to inspect Boxto. It was about 2pm and I left Barbara still cleaning the restaurant.

I opened the shutters of Boxto and peered inside to be greeted by the usual sight of half filled glasses on the sticky bar, empty bottles, cigarette butts and lots of other miscellaneous rubbish scattered around the floor. The loos were something else with the floors covered in soggy paper with the ladies basin stuffed half full with god knows what. This was normal and anyone who tries to tell you that men's toilets are worse to clean the ladies has never had to do the job. Ladies toilets are always ten times messier than the gents. God knows what they do in there.

This time I did not start to clean the place and walked back to the Dom Miguel where Barbara was polishing the glasses.

'Can I show you something?' I said quietly.

'Show me what?' replied Barbara

'Just come with me for a bit. It'll only take a minute', I said.

Still not happy with me for having a go at Steve she grudgingly followed me back towards Boxto.

I opened the door and let Barbara go inside.

Her face turned to thunder as she digested the devastation in front of her and without speaking she set off back to the apartment. I followed behind trying to keep up with her smirking to myself.

What happened next was worth paying money to see.

It was about 3pm when she opened the apartment door and screamed into the room.

'Get up now the lot of you, get up there and get that place cleaned up you lazy sods'.

She didn't have to repeat the polite request. Within seconds the four of them jumped out of their beds, quickly dressed and were running out of the door heading for Boxto.

'See what I mean', I said to Barbara.

She didn't reply but I knew she had finally got the message at last.

That night in the restaurant we had another slight disaster. Near the far wall a young couple were enjoying a meal when they both jumped out of their seats. Water was dripping onto their table from the ceiling above. I quickly moved them to another table and apologised. Luckily they had just finished their main courses.

Big Ron from the 'Pig' rented the apartment above the restaurant and I ran up the stairs next door and knocked on his door.

Big Ron answered the door. 'What's up?' he said surprised to see me standing there.

'You've got a leak, it's dripping onto our customers downstairs'.

Big Ron rushed into the bathroom and kitchen to check the taps.

'Looks OK', said Ron, 'Must be under the floor. Let me get hold of the president of the building and we'll come and have a look'.

By now the restaurant was quite busy and we had cordoned off the area affected by the dripping water.

Into the restaurant walked the president with big Ron close behind. The president was a big, beefy chap wearing a dirty vest which did not cover his stomach accompanied by the biggest set of dirty shorts, probably the biggest slob I have ever seen in my life.

My wife Barbara took the horrors at this sight, saying to Ron, 'Get him out of here now, he's dirty. We've got customers in here'.

Ron looked at her without speaking while the slob trundled around the tables inspecting the damage.

Thankfully the president quickly nodded to myself and Ron saying, 'Seguro...insurance' as he waddled out of the door.

Big Ron was not happy with Barbara's reaction to the president's dress sense or hygiene.

'Sort it out yourself next time', he said as he left following his mate, the president.

To be fair the next day the problem had been fixed.

One idea we attempted during this time was for Katy's sister, Vicky, to provide some entertainment in the restaurant, especially during the early evening period to attract customers inside. Vicky was an excellent singer and was also a bit of a comedian being able to involve customers in her act. She was performing three nights a week at a local club called '7' not far from Boxto and was really pulling in the crowds there.

Her first performance went down a storm and the restaurant was buzzing even attracting customers just to sit at the bar to drink and watch her act.

At the end of the night as I was closing up I had a visit from big Ron.

'The president is not happy', said Ron, who had actually been watching some of the performance.

'He's told me that he will raise a denuncia against you, because of the noise, and you don't have the proper license for live music.'

'Some of the other bar owners are also not happy as you will take business away from them'.

'Which bars?' I asked.

'The Spanish bars', replied Ron.

'Miserable bastards, they like telling tales don't they', I replied.

That was Vicky's one and only performance at the restaurant.

During late July with no explanation Katy did not turn up for work at the Dom Miguel. Luckily Steve came to the rescue again and he saved the day turning up the next night with another of his many temporary staff looking for a steadier stream of income. This time it was Lori a young English girl who became the fifth different waitress we had employed within four months.

It was about this time that Everaldo announced he was finishing at the end of the month to go back to Brazil. Luckily now I was not too concerned as I felt I could handle the restaurant myself without his help and he knew it and I also knew I could employ someone much cheaper to replace him. He had over the past few weeks started to become a little lazy and managed to hand the job of pulling the tables and chairs from the terrace back into the restaurant at the end of the evening to myself.

The final weekend in July was the annual Fuengirola fiesta which went on for a few days at the local 'Feria' ground where the weekly market used to be held in the centre of Fuengirola.

The highlight of the weekend was a march around the streets of Fuengirola, the main theme being countries of the world with the separate groups dressed in National costumes and playing country specific music.

The finale was the Saturday evening when the groups headed for the Feria ground where the empty shop units had been converted into themed bars representing each country with entertainment being performed inside each bar.

Myself and Barbara visited a few of the bars, which were packed solid and enjoyed the music from Brazil, the samba dancing from Cuba, flamenco from Spain, Cossack dancing from Russia. It was a brilliant night of free entertainment and the place was buzzing.

Our final stop was to the UK bar which was surprisingly quiet. The theme took a while to understand. At the front there was a stage with four or five guys doing a Morris dance and the floor in front was supposed to represent a wartime Naafi with a load of wooden trestles and chairs, all completely bare with no attempt at any level of decoration.

Behind a small bar sat a chap dressed as what looked to me like World Cup Willie from the 1966 world cup and a woman dressed like one of Cinderella's ugly sisters with a union jack wrapped around her shoulders.

That was it, very proud to be British that night.

The last day in July my car arrived from the UK and Barbara and I walked towards the Lidl store where we had arranged to pick it up that morning.

We arrived to find the transporter wagon ready and waiting for us and the car was handed over.

I remember driving the car into Lidl to do the normal shop and feeling ecstatic that I did not have to carry the shopping the mile or so back to the restaurant. Now without the scooter it was an absolute godsend.

The kids had all gone back to the UK now and we sat down with Steve again and Mikey to discuss what more we could do to help Botxo.

I asked Mikey if he would take charge of Boxto as although Steve could run the bar to put on theme nights etc his skills were not suited to the more mundane tasks such as managing the money, ordering stock or last but not least the cleaning. His talents lay in front of house activities and of course sleeping. Steve was not too happy with this arrangement but really was not in a great position to challenge the decision.

I also asked Mikey to change his DJ name to something more exotic. I mean 'Mikey the DJ' does not conjure up hip images like 'Judge Jules' or 'Booka Shade', it sounds more like a kids entertainer. I don't think he was too impressed with my suggestion as he uttered 'I'll think about it', whilst shaking his head. I personally thought my request was quite reasonable.

Myself and Barbara now we had the car went looking for half a dozen tables and some chairs to stick on the terrace of Boxto and bought strings of coloured lights to brighten up the entrance and generally make the place more attractive to customers. Mikey, who was a builder by trade in a previous life also agreed to re tile the terrace which had lots of broken tiles.

Inside the bar we bought candles and more lights to brighten the place up and moved some of the high stools from the restaurant to line the bar in Boxto.

One key decision we made was to try and secure the services of a young guy from London called Ross who had the reputation of being king of the hundreds of PR's patrolling the front pulling in customers by the bucketload for a competitor's bar.

At the time we had some friends from the UK visiting and one night Barbara and her friend Debbie grabbed and dragged Ross from outside Botxo inside and wouldn't let him go until he agreed to work for us, threatening to beat him up if he wouldn't agree. I don't think Ross had ever been threatened by two fifty year old women before and eventually had to agree. He was also offered free food at the restaurant which he took advantage of only a couple of times over the next few weeks. Finally we employed a young geordie guy, a small bald chap called Johnny who was just a bundle of energy and would be a huge asset in the bar and he was fluent in Spanish.

One story about Johnny which sticks vividly in my mind was an episode during August on probably one of the hottest days of the year. It was mid afternoon and as usual I was returning to the apartment for my afternoon kip ready for my shift at the restaurant.
As I walked into the apartment I decided to have a quick cigarette on the balcony before hitting the sack.
Standing looking over the balcony towards the sea there was a small movement to my right.
It was Johnny, lying in the corner looking like a roasted lobster and for the first time the normally bubbly and chatty individual could hardly speak.
It unravelled that he had come back to the apartment with Steve and fell asleep on the balcony. Steve who had obviously forgotten about him had locked the patio doors and shuffled off to bed.

The sun up to late afternoon hits the balcony full on with no shade at all and Johnny despite banging on the doors and shouting to passing people below from the 5th floor had been left to frazzle to the point of near death. I never saw him at the apartment again funnily enough, but he did recover in time.

During August things picked up slightly, but it was obvious we had just about lost the original Spanish customer base from Boxto apart from a few Spanish kids who never spent any money in the bar. Luckily the young Brits had arrived and Ross was pulling them into Boxto.

Steve was his usual upbeat self but one morning as usual I checked his bedroom and he was not there. Slightly worried I walked up towards Boxto to find him half asleep sitting on a bench on the seafront.

'Are you OK?' I said to Steve. 'Get yourself to bed'.

Steve was obviously still quite affected by his previous night's drinking session and slurred back to me.

'Yesssh fine', he replied with a spaced out look on his face.

An old Spanish chap approached us and sat down on the bench beside us listening to the conversation when he suddenly produced a 20 cents coin and handed it to Steve before walking off.

'He thinks I'm a tramp', said Steve.

'Wonder why', I replied. 'Think you had better go and sleep it off now, or you could just sit here and collect some more cash. It would help pay your bills'.

Steve unsteadily stood up and set off towards the apartment.

Fuengirola is not a great place to be wandering the streets late at night. Most of the Spanish youth carry knives and there are lots of Moroccans looking for easy pickings.

The Moroccans work by coming up to you and putting their arms around you then shouting something like, 'Ah you English, I love you', followed by, 'Wayne Rooney, David Beckham, Tony Blair', while at the same time wrapping their right leg around yours in order to push you to the ground to mug you.

I was always very wary of this when out late at night and on one occasion a young Moroccan chap was coming directly towards me with his arms stretched out in front of him ready for his planned 'cuddle'.

Before he could touch me I shouted very loudly at him, 'Do not fucking touch me, keep your bloody hands to yourself, you thieving bastard'.

This seemed to catch him very much by surprise as he stepped back looking puzzled at why I had reacted in this way before moving on.

One night very late in the restaurant an English guy called Stuart aged around 25 rushed up to the bar in a state of panic and sweating profusely. He had eaten in the restaurant earlier in the evening with two of his mates.

'I think I've bloody killed them', he said breathing heavily.

'Killed who?' I asked.

'Two guys attacked me and pushed me to the ground, trying to get hold of my wallet', said Stuart.

'Are you OK?' I said pouring him a drink to calm him down.

"Yes, I'm fine but I beat the shit out of them. I think I've killed them'.

'Good for you', I replied, 'Two less of the bastards to worry about'.

'Yes, I used to be a light heavyweight boxing champion in the Navy a few years ago', said Stuart.

By then a couple of other Brits had arrived listening to what was going on. Stuart had now reached hero status and had free drinks bought for him for the rest of the night.

The next night word spread around Fish Alley that the Town Hall chaps were on the prowl looking at valid work permits.

Karen from the restaurant further down the street, dashed into the Dom Miguel with a look of panic on her face.

'Phil, they are down the street coming this way to check the work permits', she said. 'Come here look'.

I looked down the street and outside the Aviva restaurant about fifty metres down the street I could see all of their restaurant staff lined up against the wall being interrogated by the Town Hall inspectors and the local police.

I dashed back into the restaurant and asked Lori, who was paid cash in hand, to leave now before they arrived.

Hamed piped up, 'Phil, my contract only covers ten hours a week. If they find me here they may ask some awkward questions and do me for more tax. I'd better leave as well. Halima can cope for a bit'.

'OK, but don't go far. I need you back here as soon as possible', I replied.

The entire street was buzzing and Dave owner of the Spanish Sunshine cafe appeared at the door.

'Aviva's been done, three staff with no contracts', he said.

The inspectors must have at that point decided that they had done enough for one night and left Fish Alley without any further checks.

Rodrigo who had been part owner of Boxto when it was sold to me also part owned the Aviva restaurant and was summoned to court the next week and fined very heavily. Couldn't have happened to a nicer chap as you will discover later in the book.

Ross was pulling the Brits into Boxto as usual but at the back of my mind I knew that they would all soon be going home as the summer ended.

Boxto started picking up at the weekends especially and we were again just about on track to meet the bills despite the best efforts of the water authority who without any notice one day decided to switch off the water to Boxto.

Carlos as usual rescued the situation who informed us that we owed the water company 300 euros. The bill hadn't been paid since February.

I found out later that there was a post box for Boxto at the end of one of the pizza takeaways at the bottom of the street alongside about a dozen other boxes. When I discovered it the box was stuffed full of bills and random other letters dating back about two years.

Clearing up in the restaurant one night just before starting our late meal suddenly Steve burst into through the doors in a panic.

'Dad, the police are at Boxto they want to speak to the owner. You will have to come now'.

I immediately jumped up, told Barbara to stay and finish off in the restaurant and hurried with Steve towards Boxto.

No one was inside Boxto and one of the guys from a neighbouring club shouted over to me.

'He's in there', pointing to a small pizza bar.

I looked across and there sitting on the cafe terrace by himself stuffing his face with pizza and drinking beer was a very fat policeman with a Mexican moustache dressed in green.

Now in Spain there are two types of cop. Those dressed in blue are the town cops who are almost human and those dressed in green the Guardia Civil, the notorious military police who are not.

My heart sank as I had heard about their reputation for being slightly corrupt to say the least as I walked over the road to where he was sitting. Try typing in Guardia Civil and the word corrupt on Google you may be surprised.

'Hola...do you speak English?' I enquired.

The fat cop took a bite out of his pizza and looked directly at me.

'Yes, I speak English', he said. 'I look after you...any trouble I will look after you'.

'Thanks', I said, 'Great'.

'40 euros a week and you will have no trouble', said the fat cop. 'It is not safe around here without me to help you. You pay me here every week'.

One of the other owners of one of the clubs came across the road.

'We all have to pay', he said. 'They can make things very difficult if you don't pay you will be closed down without any reason. Even the Town Hall can do nothing to stop this lot'.

'Si, you all pay, I make sure you have no trouble', said the cop taking another bite of what was obviously his free pizza.

Now you may think that I had the misfortune to come across one bent cop in Fuengirola but every week from then on I handed over the 40 euros to different corrupt 'green' individuals whose turn it was to collect that week. Obviously due to the cost of living this figure increased to 50 euros at the turn of the following year.
I did however receive some invaluable advice from Antonio, my abogado...'Just pay them what they ask', he said.

I handed over the 40 euros and went back to the restaurant.

'Even the cops are bloody bent', I said to Barbara as I explained what had just happened.

'You shouldn't have come here, should you', she replied.

'Bloody right I shouldn't', I responded.

At the end of the month Lori told me that she was planning to leave on exactly the same day that Everaldo was due to go back to Brazil and despite my pleas to go a few days later so that she could help with handover to Everaldo's replacement she was insistent that she was going.

Like I mentioned previously it was fairly easy to recruit serving staff in the restaurant and I recruited quickly a young Danish girl called Carin and a young Finnish chap called Adar. Both could speak both Spanish and English. By this time I had to let the young Irish PR go due to his time keeping but more because his ironing skills were lacking and he actually did turn up on the night I sacked him in a wet crumpled shirt literally put on straight out of the washing machine, still damp.

I had decided anyway that the PR job should be my responsibility and I became a little more confident in approaching customers looking at the menu to drag them through the door.

On the night Everaldo left we all had a drink and thanked him for his fantastic help in the early days for which we were very grateful.

He turned to me as he was leaving and said, 'Phil, you have learnt well, in six months you will be the biggest bastard restaurateur in Fuengirola'. He knew that I had no reliance on him any more.

'What do you mean by that?' I replied

'You will know when it has happened', said Everaldo.

Carin and Adar were excellent recruits and Adar was telepathic in being able to spot Finnish tourists passing by, although he hated the majority of them for some reason.

There are apparently two classes of people in Finland, those from Helsinki who were OK according to Adar and those from 'the forest' who were subhuman according to him. He refused point blank to engage with those from 'the forest' who he could somehow spot from a distance without even speaking to them.

The day after Everaldo left I went with Steve for a quick drink in the bar owned by Karen and Barry called Raw and I was telling her that in four months I was now on my sixth and seventh lot of waiting staff.

'Think yourself lucky', said Karen. 'We are on our third chef now and the two before him were very average. Waiting staff are easy to get, a good chef is impossible to find around here. We are selling the restaurant and opening a small cafe bar on the front. Barry has volunteered to do the cooking'.

'Can't imagine Barry wearing an apron', I replied.

'He doesn't know yet', said Karen. 'It's about time he did some hard work'.

A few days later Barry wandered into the Dom Miguel saying that his chef had without any notice not turned up but the sale of the restaurant was going through and they would be moving to the new place in six weeks.

'What about a chef till then?' I said.

'Were just running it as a bar till we move', said Barry.

'We could do snacks for you and deliver them from next door. Just burgers, chips and stuff like that if you like. It might make the customers stay and buy a few more drinks', I said.

'Ok, let's give it a try', said Barry. 'Knock up a quick menu'.

I was pleased with the possibility of doing a bit more business but it left a deep impression with me that my business was totally reliant on keeping Hamed happy which concerned me.

A few days later Barry, Karen and Dave came rushing into the restaurant early in the evening.

'Phil', said Dave, 'We've been talking to Gordon Ramsey's crew. They are doing a series about Spanish restaurants and looking for volunteers. It's called Kitchen Nightmares and Ramsey turns up to help you sort out the restaurant and make you loads of money'.

'We've told them that you will do it and they are coming here tonight to talk to you', continued Dave.

'Tonight', I replied, 'Oh go on then what is there to lose it should be a laugh', I said.

I shouted Hamed across and asked him if he was OK with this.

'No problem', I have seen Ramsey on the TV', said Hamed. 'I will look forward to teaching him'.

'You have to pretend you can't cook by the way', I said to Hamed.

'Ok, no problem, I will look forward to seeing them', he replied.

That night two pretentious looking guys turned up carrying a camera and sound boom with a young girl following behind.

'Want a drink?' I said

'OK three cokes please', replied the young girl.

I poured the drinks and asked for four euros. The young girl looked surprised to be asked for payment for the drinks obviously thinking they were for free'.

'More than I will take tonight', I said, 'Every little helps'.

The restaurant was quite full at the time and I had told all of the customers as they sat down that the Ramsey crew were coming in and to say that the food was rubbish if they were asked. They were well up for it.

'Not a problem', they all replied looking forward to the entertainment.

The crew had me stood behind the bar pointing the camera at me with a sound boom being held above my head ready for my interview.

The young girl kicked it off.

'So how is business in the Dom Miguel and what are your main problems?'

'Terrible', I replied. 'I have no experience of running a restaurant and could do with some help in here'.

'OK so what exactly are the biggest issues you have', the girl continued.

'The food I think', I replied, 'There are always problems', I lied looking in the direction of Hamed who was listening just inside the kitchen.

'It's the food really....not cooked properly....orders missing. We are all over the place'.

Hamed was trying to listen and I had to retain my serious expression for the camera.

I looked towards the closest table where a young couple were sitting. They noticed me looking at them and on cue started prodding the food and shaking their heads. The interviewer noticed this as I also shook my head saying 'See what I mean'.

'And why do you think that Gordon Ramsey could help you?' said the young girl.

'Well I have run a restaurant for only six months and I guess he has run restaurants for 30 years. I figure he must know quite a bit more than I do', I replied.
Dave and Karen arrived and were stood by the bar now listening quite amused by the conversation.

'Can we speak to your chef?' the girl continued.

'Yes, but don't tell him what I have been saying about the food. I need to keep him here until I can find someone better', I replied. 'And for no more than 5 minutes, if you don't mind. He is working and he is bad enough without being disturbed by you lot'.

'Ok, fine, I won't', she replied as I shouted into the kitchen for Hamed to be interviewed.

I left Hamed with the film crew and walked across to where Dave, Karen and Barry were standing by the bar.

'Cracked it', I said. 'He'll definitely be coming'.

Hamed wrapped up his interview and returned to the kitchen.

'What do you think? Is he going to help us...what are our chances?' I said to the girl.

'Still some more restaurants to see', she replied. 'Definitely possible'.

As they left I spoke to Hamed.

'What did you say?'

'Bad service, all about bad service. Told them you were useless', he said.

'What did you say about the food?' I asked.

'Said the food was fine...told them it's all your fault'.

'I told them the food was rubbish', I replied laughing.

We both laughed as we finished our nights work.

Never did hear from Ramsey's lot again.

In the middle of August we had a regular mugging in Boxto. On this occasion like many others it was the Moroccans. Mikey, Steve's DJ had his mobile phone lifted while we was busily organising his nightly playlists. A young Moroccan chap picked up his phone from behind the decks and took off towards the door.

Mikey shouted after the thief and Mikey, his brother Des and Steve all ran after him catching him a short distance up the street.

Mikey asked for the phone to be returned and was a little bemused when the chap rather than just handing him back the phone and remove the strong possibility of being beaten up by three strapping guys started shouting. 'My phone now, you lost it, it's my phone'.

Reasoning with him was impossible and as he attempted to run off again he was quickly dropped to the ground with Mikey and Des sat on his stomach desperately trying to pull the phone from his hand.

The Moroccan chap still refused to hand over the phone continuing his rant that the phone was now his property.

A final quick stamp on his arm finally released his grip and Mikey was able to retrieve his phone.

The guy who obviously had a bit of a death wish started shouting, 'Stop, thieves, my phone', as Mikey, Des and Steve walked back to Boxto.

The guy honestly was under the impression that the phone was his now because it was in his possession even though he knew he had nicked it. Unbelievable.

You will probably be able to see this chap along with his mates on the Costa del Crime television series played out two years later. Boxto and the clubs in the same area were always a regular feature on the programme.

During the second week of August, on my Monday night off I went for a meal with Barbara to discuss the point we had reached and what to do next.

Looking at Boxto first. It clearly was not making any money and even now in August we would be struggling to pay the bills. We had lost the Spanish customers and were now reliant on Ross and his PR mates to get anyone into the place to spend money, chiefly the young Brits.

We had cut costs a little now and decided not to employ a bouncer who was quite expensive and not really needed as we did not have customers clamouring to get into Boxto.

We agreed that the Brits holiday season would soon be over and Ross, Mikey the DJ and other PR guys over for the summer would be going home soon.

Next we looked at the Dom Miguel. We were now breaking even but only managing to fill covers out on the terrace. It was very difficult to persuade customers to sit inside the restaurant. Barbara was also suffering with back problems due to the constant bending etc cleaning and serving in the restaurant.

Finally, we are totally reliant on the chef, if he leaves that's it !!!, and finally I don't think I can trust anyone over here.

All of our savings were invested in the two businesses.

'What about you going back to the UK?' I asked, 'See if you can get your old job back if it hasn't been filled'.

'That's what I was thinking', she replied, 'At least we will have some guaranteed income'.

'We need to sell Boxto now, it will get much worse in the winter when the tourists have all gone home, I'll put it up for sale tomorrow'.

'Why not sell them both?' said Barbara. 'The restaurant isn't doing anything either and you are working 18 hours a day, it'll bloody kill you'.

'You're right', I replied. 'Let's take a hit on Boxto and put it for sale cheap and up the sale price on the Dom Miguel to cover the loss on Boxto. See if have any offers. Nothing to lose is there, and we don't have to sell'.

'Right let's do it', said Barbara.

The next day Barbara rang the hospital where she had worked and begged for her job back.

After a stern talking to from her ex boss and lots of grovelling she managed to get her to agree that she could start again the following Monday morning.

Barbara had lasted six weeks of her new life in the sun, living the dream and left Fuengirola on the Sunday afternoon.

I rang a local business estates office, Fiesta Properties and arranged for discrete viewings of Boxto and the Dom Miguel. Botxo was put on the market for 20,000 euros, 35,000 euros below the buying price and the Dom Miguel was priced at 166,000 euros, 56,000 euros above the buying price. Taking into account fees and 20% payments to the landlord I figured this would just about give us just about a break even figure. However, most importantly the sale had to remain a secret particularly from Hamed, the chef.

Stuart, the agent from Fiesta Properties arrived at the restaurant with his camera to take photos for his web site.

'I want 166,000 euros for the Dom Miguel and 20,000 for Boxto', I said to Stuart. 'I don't care what you add on top for your commission'.

'OK, no problem', he replied as he finished off taking all of the details.

During the last week in August, two important events happened.

Firstly, it was noticeable that the Spanish tourists had all returned to their lives inland and the golfers began to arrive in Fuengirola, particularly the Irish.

One day as I was busy as usual with my bucket and mop bleaching the terrace a couple of young Irish guys called Calum and Mark walked past and we started chatting.

'Hi there', said Mark. 'We're looking for somewhere to have our trophy presentation evening. Where's good around here?'

'You've found it', I replied in anticipation.

'There's 21 of us', said Mark

'No problem and I can promise you free champagne. I can also guarantee that I have the best chef in Fuengirola, he was trained in Paris. If you don't like the food the chef will caddy for you free for a week'.

Calum was looking at the menu.

'They do fillet steaks', he said. 'That will keep most of the guys happy'.

They walked into the restaurant.

'Can you fit 21 in here, we all want to sit together and we want a table to present the trophies', said Calum.

I thought quickly pointing to the tables showing how I could arrange them as one long table running the length of the restaurant with a table positioned just behind for the trophies.

'Right, let's do it, around 8.30, Thursday….don't forget the champagne', said Calum.

'Excellent', I replied, 'Can you take a couple of menus and drop in the orders before Thursday. I don't want to upset the chef and we can have everything ready for when you arrive'.

'No problem. I'll drop them in this afternoon', said Calum. 'By the way before I forget make sure you have lots of Jamesons whisky and Faustino wine as well'.

Fantastic result I said to myself and couldn't wait to tell Hamed.

Before the big night I stocked up on Faustino wine and Jameson's whiskey as promised and bought five bottles of champagne, Spanish Cava of course at three euros a bottle and bought extra steak fillet and rump from Macro the day before. All from the a la carte menu with no Menu del Dia to even think about.

On the Thursday evening at around 6pm myself and Adar arranged the tables and Carin laid the cutlery and glasses ready for the group to arrive. For some reason early evening was busier than usual and we had already served around thirty covers before the Irish arrived.

At around 08.15 we placed the five bottles of Cava in ice buckets spaced evenly down the long table and at 08.30 on the dot the guys arrived. Calum set out the trophies on the table and the drinking began. Quickly the champagne was gone and I was inundated with orders for triple vodkas and red bull in pint glasses, six bottles of Faustino, pint after pint of San Miguel and lots of other concoctions.

The starters all arrived on time and were devoured in seconds by the group. Hamed was working at a fast pace to deliver the 21 mains, mainly steaks in one go all done to different requirements. 2 blue steaks, 8 rare, 4 medium rare 5 medium, 2 well done all delivered perfectly to the table.

After the mains were cleared Mark stood up and made the presentations while Carin stood by picking up extra drinks orders which were still coming thick and fast.

At the end of the presentations Mark asked me to bring out the chefs to meet the guys and as Hamed and Halima appeared they were given a rapturous round of applause by the group.

'Where are the others?' said Mark.

'No it's just the two of them', I replied.

'Bloody well can't believe they managed to do that lot', replied Mark.

Hamed and Halima suitably embarrassed returned to the safety of the kitchen but no doubt were feeling high as kites.

The guys finished off their meals, with coffee and triple rounds of Jamesons whisky ready for their night on the town at around 11.30.

I totted up the bill ...1260 euros and passed it to Calum.

'Right lads that works out at 60 euros each for the meal. I'll put a bit extra in, plus 10 euros each tip....70 euros each', said Calum to the group.

The guys scrambled in their wallets and soon there was a mound of cash covering the table.

Calum checked the money and handed over the cash, handing the 210 euro tip to Carin with a big hug.

'Fantastic night', said Mark as they all got up to leave each one thanking myself, Carin and Adar in turn and waving to Hamed and Halima as they went out of the door.

At the end of the night I counted the takings...1650 euros...four times more than a usual night. Can't wait to tell Barb. What a night.

From the highs of the night before the next night was a complete nightmare. The extractor fan in the kitchen decided to have a siesta and broke down. Now, we are not talking about an extractor you would find in your standard household kitchen but an industrial strength beast about two metres by three metres running the length of the kitchen fitted above the gas cooking rings and two large ovens.

With the extractor working I personally would be able to just about cope with the heat generated in the windowless kitchen for about one hour. How Hamed and Halima coped with the heat in mid summer for six hours I will never know but apart from Hamed drinking two full two litre bottles of water each shift he never ever mentioned the heat. With no extractor fan it was a different story with the heat from the ovens added to the steam from the huge industrial dish washing equipment the kitchen was a sauna. They were really struggling.

The next day I spoke to the landlord, Alberto, to see if he knew anyone who could fix the problem, which he did and rang his contact on my behalf to arrange for him to come the next day.

The engineer arrived as promised on time and borrowed my step ladder to climb up into the roofspace running directly above the extractor unit.

He could speak little English and after ten minutes checking the unit he asked me to join him in the loft space. Shining his torch he pointed to what looked like some sort of power unit sitting inside a metal box with the lid undone.

'Kaput', he said pointing to the power unit.

I nodded my head and went ahead of him back down the ladder towards the bar.

'Cuanto cuesta...how much?' I asked.

He wrote down on a piece of paper, 1500 euros ....tres dias..dos a ordanar...uno completo..

I repeated in English, 'Three days, two days to order unit and one day to fit'.

He nodded back to me.

'OK, do it', I said and he left the restaurant.

That afternoon I bought two electric fans which I thought would help the situation in the kitchen until the new unit was fitted.

Hamed on arriving that night picked up the fans and threw them back out of the kitchen.

'No, these just make a hot wind', said Hamed. 'No good'.

He managed to finish the shift but as he left he really was not looking too happy and was completely drained. I needed to do something quick to stop the situation going on for another two nights or I would have to close the restaurant.

The next day without any real hope I walked into town to speak to the company who dealt with my refrigerator maintenance, 'Servicio Maquinas', to see if they could help me.

I explained to the chap that I needed a new power unit for the extractor fan and wondered if they might have one in stock.

'My guys are due to do the fridge maintenance next week anyway. I will ask them to come tonight instead and they can find out what unit is needed', he said.

The two engineers who had serviced the fridges a couple of times before arrived at 5pm just as Hamed arrived at the restaurant and began to speak about the problem to Hamed.

Soon the taller chap was climbing the ladders into the roofspace.

Suddenly there was the best noise I could have hoped for. The fans started whirring in the kitchen as the extractor came back to life.

The service chap appeared at the hatch to the ceiling.

'Just a fuse', he said.

'What about the unit?' I said

'No, very new', he replied. 'It's ok'.

'You do need to get the filters cleaned in the extractor or the fuse might blow again. We can take them away and clean them and bring them back tomorrow', said the service engineer.

'How much?' I enquired.

'Oh, five euros for the fuse and twenty euros to clean the filters', he replied.

'Hamed, is it OK to take the filters?' I said.

'Yes, no problem the extractor will work OK without them for tonight'.

The two guys removed the six filters from the unit ready to leave.

'How long should it be before the filters need to be cleaned?' I asked.

'Every two months', the chap replied. 'We can add it to your contract if you want'.

'Great', I replied 'and thanks for fixing the problem with the fan'.

I was really relieved as I picked up the phone to ring the landlord, Alberto.

I explained what had happened and rather than being pleased he was upset saying that his mate was honest and the service guys I had used did not know what they were doing.

'Tell him to just cancel his order', I said while he was muttering away and I put the phone down on him mid mutter.

Another big decision I had to make at this time was the new smoking guidelines issued by the Spanish government which had to be in place in two weeks. This was the hottest topic of conversation among all of the restaurant owners and we all felt that if we banned smoking from the restaurants all of our businesses would go down the pan.

We had two choices. We could make the restaurant completely smoke free or we could section off an area inside just for smokers but we had to make sure that non smokers could not pass through this forbidden area on their way to the bar or the loos etc.

It was a real dilemma and we were all panic stricken with the news as at the time smoking in restaurants was still allowed in the UK so obviously the Brits, my main customers were not used to it.

One night while working in the restaurant I noticed a couple of Irish guys who would leave their table inside, walk outside and light up their cigarettes in the street.

I spoke to the two guys as they returned to their tables.

'Why do you go outside to smoke?' I asked.

'Oh', the guy replied, 'Just habit, been doing it without really thinking. We haven't been able to smoke in restaurants or bars back home in Ireland for six months now'.

'And doesn't it bother you?' I asked

'No, not at all. I prefer to eat in a smoke free area anyway', the Irish guy replied.

I explained the dilemma I was now facing.

'Go no smoking', they both said.' Honest you will have no problems. Customers can always sit on the terrace or step outside for a fag'.

That was it decision made, I would go no smoking inside, and it was very much the right decision. In the rest of the time I was running the restaurant there was only one occasion when a customer sat down and decided to leave when he realised it was non smoking. On the other hand the number of customers who put their heads in the door to check we were non smoking before entering ran into the fifties.

By law we had to display signs around the restaurant showing that we were clearly non smoking which I dutifully had printed off from my local print shop.

This did not stop Bonnie and Clyde from the town hall, the two guys who were paranoid about my chairs being a couple of inches over the red line on my terrace arriving and complaining that my signs were too small. They had to be exactly 25.4 centimetres by 20.32 centimetres and not the 20.32 by 20.32 centimetres that I had had the gall to display inside and outside of my restaurant.

I offered to stick one on top of the other to make them 40 centimetres square which would show two no smoking messages instead of only one as they stood tape measures in hand.

They were not open to my suggestion and issued me with their compliance ticket. You couldn't make it up ...two bloody inches.

I found it incredibly funny that in Spain, important things like for instance like paying tax and honestly submitting property sale prices were not a high priority but silly little rules had to be obeyed at all costs. God forbid your chairs are a couple of inches over the line. Will the Spanish economy ever go down the pan?...I wonder.

Taking Off Now

At the end of August beginning of September things began to change dramatically in the restaurant. The Spanish tourists had to a large extent disappeared thank god, and the older Brits were now arriving as the temperatures cooled and the nights started to draw in. Business was picking up as British customers tend to eat their evening meals much earlier than the Spanish.

The numbers inside the restaurant were increasing and the daily taking ramped up to around 750 euros a night. I was at last making a healthy profit but this created an unforeseen problem.

At the end of a busy service, the third in a row, Hamed who had not been in a particularly good mood all night stormed out of the restaurant shouting as he went.

'Fuck this, I am not working like a dog anymore, I am fed up with preparing fresh vegetables...menu too bloody big...that's it ..I'm finished with you...I'm not coming back'.

'What?' I replied.

Hamed ignored me and stormed out of the door.

'That's it...no more..I go somewhere else', he shouted.

'Shit', I thought to myself if Hamed goes that's it.

The next day I woke up very worried not knowing if Hamed would be back that night and I left half a dozen messages on his phone. He didn't respond to any.

I opened as usual at 5 feeling sick to the stomach standing by the door looking, waiting for Hamed to arrive.

Suddenly I spotted him walking towards me.

'Hamed, thank god you have come, can we sit down and sort this out?' I said desperately.

'Wait till end of shift and we will sit down', replied Hamed.

The evening, which again was quite busy, passed off quietly.

At the end of the night I sat nervously waiting for Hamed to finish his cleaning and we sat down to talk.

'Do you need more help?' I said, 'We can get more help'.

'No', said Hamed. 'You pay me more'.

'How much?' I replied.

'30 cents per customer and 15 cents for each kid', he replied.' Then the busier we are, the harder I work and the more I get paid'.

I quickly scribbled down some numbers. 30 customers equals 9 euros, 60 customers equals 18 euros for Hamed.

'Happy with that', I replied and we shook hands.

For the next few days I was thinking more and more as to how I could reduce my total reliance on Hamed and advertised for someone to help Hamed and Halima in the kitchen.

My objective was to not just find a helper but a chef who could take over from Hamed if he ever decided to leave.

I interviewed a Chinese chap called Sun who appeared to have the right credentials and I briefed him to learn as much as possible to become Hamed's deputy if needed.

Sun started in the kitchen mainly doing the less glamorous tasks dictated to by both Hamed and Halima for a couple of weeks.

At the end of the two weeks I sat down with Sun.

'Reckon you can run the kitchen, make the sauces etcetera?' I enquired.

'Sure, no problem', replied Sun.

'Great', I said, 'Let's open on Monday, Hamed's day off and I'll ask Halima to work some extra hours. I am sure she will'.

'Excellent', replied Sun looking pleased about the quick promotion.

Monday evening arrived and Sun was at the restaurant early switching on the gas and preparing for the evening ahead.

At 6pm the first customers arrived and were duly served their starters which were normally prepared by Halima.

Clearing away the plates I returned to the kitchen awaiting the main course which I expected to be ready to served.

'5 minutes', said Sun as I waited for him to plate up the food.

More customers were now arriving and I handed Sun two additional orders followed quickly by a third.

As usual the starters arrived in a short time.

'Are you ready for the mains, table 5?' I said to Sun.

'Table 5 waiting for vegetables', he replied.

'Table 3 nearly ready', replied Sun.

'Table 5 should be first. You have to get table 5 out first', I said.

In what seemed to be a lifetime but was more like 15 minutes the food arrived for table 5 which was whisked out by Carin waiting at the hatch.

More orders were arriving as Table 3 went out.

'There's a problem with Table 3', said Carin. 'The lasagne is frozen inside'.

I prodded the lasagne with my finger and it was frozen solid inside.

'Shit' I thought, and walked across to apologise to the customers on Table 3.

More customers were arriving and soon the orders were really piling up now.

I quickly grabbed Carin and Adar to tell any new customers that there would be a 30 to 45 minute wait for their meals.

Many customers turned around and walked out and for the first time I was pleased not to see customers sitting down.

Things were in complete meltdown in the kitchen as Halima was trying her best to help Sun complete the orders.

Eventually the night ended thank god and as the last customers left I sat down with Sun.

'Not great was it', I said,' Bet you learned a lot'.

'Yes', said Sun looking very stressed.

'See you tomorrow?' I asked as he left.

'Sure', he replied.

I never saw Sun again.

September was good as the numbers were consistent and seemed to be increasing. The darker nights and the deluge of Brits and Northern Europeans meant the numbers were rising to around 60 covers a night.

I decided to make a few changes.

Instead of one menu del dia priced at 7.75 for three courses I developed 3 separate menus with the help of Hamed.

We reduced the size of the original 7.75 menu del dia offering, removing steak and pork dishes from the menu, leaving a choice of chicken or pasta dishes and also removed the more expensive starters leaving three soups and a couple of the other cheap starter choices.

I reprinted the cheap menu on a fairly bland looking black and white printed sheet so as not to look overly attractive.

The next thing was to produce the second menu which now included the steak and pork dishes and re added the starters removed from the cheap menu back onto the list. I priced this menu at 9.95 euros with an additional 3 euro supplement added for the steak dishes. This menu font and colours looked very attractive and appealing.

The final change was to produce the 'Gourmet Menu del Dia'. This menu mainly packaged most of the a la carte starters, mains and desserts including choices like fillet steak, salmon and lamb chops for a price of 18 euros for the three courses again with a 3 euro supplement for the steak.

Within days sales of the cheap menu had virtually disappeared and the new 9.95 menu was selling fast, although I did lose one of my very few regular Spanish customers who were horrified at the price increases. The gourmet menu was selling at around three per night also.

I had now increased the takings per cover which with drinks included rose from around 12 euros per head to around 16 euros per head.

I was now filling the restaurant every night with regular takings averaging over 1,000 euros most nights.

I was determined now to make as much money as possible from the restaurant but still determined to sell the place as soon as possible.

At this point I realised it was unfair to place the burden of pulling customers into the restaurant on the service staff. It was my restaurant, my problem and my responsibility to do this and not sit complaining and blaming others for not doing it. It was about time I practised what I was preaching and stop being such a complete tart.

This determination overcame my original fear of trying to pull customers from outside looking at the menus into the restaurant. After a few trials I became expert at pulling in enough customers early in the service to hit the quarter full target which I set for 8pm. Remember the quote, a restaurant quarter full means a full restaurant as customers are attracted to busy restaurants.

Over the next few weeks I perfected my techniques for pulling in the customers and in the end it just became part of the job.

First rule was to never stand beside and hover over customers who were looking at the menu. They become uncomfortable and just want to move on if they feel they are being harassed with you standing over them.

The best thing to do if you see customers at the menus which were positioned at the edge of the outside terrace is to casually walk to the door of the restaurant leaving a ten foot distance between you and the customers and not to stray onto the terrace itself.

Then I learned a number of interchangeable ways of engaging the customers at the menu in an unthreatening way depending on how full the restaurant was.

Common ways to engage was to use the following chat up lines.

Number one....just casually say things like. 'Great food in here, best down this street'. The normal response is for the customers to look up and say something like...'Yes you would say that wouldn't you, bet you own the place', laughing.

My response would be a couple of things...

'Look if you don't like it you can have the meal for half price. My chef is fantastic'.

or it could be if they were British it might be ' Where are you from?' I would ask.

They would reply with Manchester or Yorkshire or wherever'

'God you have chosen the right night'. Free glass of wine tonight for everyone from Manchester or Yorkshire or Timbuktu for that matter if that is where they said they were from.

or even I would say…. 'Don't leave us until the last day of your holiday because I know you will want to come back here again for a second time'.

Probably the best ice breaker I used every night would be as I stood by the door which worked to pull in many customers involved the sausages.

I mentioned previously that we were now selling Big Willeys sausages in the restaurant who was a renowned British butcher in Fuengirola who had posters pinned up all over town.

As potential customers were looking at the menu I would shout across the terrace. 'We've got Big Willeys in here, no one else in Fuengirola has…..have you ever had a Big Willey?', referring to Big Willeys sausages on the menu, of course. This would always without fail amuse the ladies who nine times out of ten would respond with something along the lines of.

'Never had a big Willey. I wouldn't know', looking at their husbands with a disappointed look on their faces.

'Well you will get three of them in here for 8 euros', I would always reply. Ice now broken you could then talk them through the door with the offer of a free glass of wine.

The best tip to attract customers was to use the regulars who had been in the restaurant before and who I already had a good relationship with.

The terrace was about six metres wide and two metres deep with a menu placed at each corner of the terrace facing the street.

I always placed the first customers at the two tables beside each of the menus offering them a free glass of wine.

After clearing their starters I made an extra point of asking them how their meals had been. If they responded positively the conversation always went as follows.

'Yes, I've got a great chef here wait until you try the mains', I would say. 'If you mention how good the food is to people looking at the menu, I will give you a free drink of your choice'.

Sometimes these customers would do this as a challenge and begin talking to people looking at the menu looking to persuade them to come in.

If I saw that they were not speaking to the potential customers I would make an excuse to go up to the table to check everything was OK with their meals. While talking to them I would casually say something like, 'The food is great in here, isn't it', making sure that the people looking at the menu could hear me talking to them.

I would then turn towards the people viewing the menu and say something like 'Best chef in Fuengirola here, if you don't believe me ask these', nodding towards the customers who were sat down eating their meals.

They always responded with comments like 'Yes, really good food', which hooked them to come in.

I even had some regulars who came to the restaurant just to sit at these two tables and do my PR for me. For a few shots of brandy this was money well spent.

As I became more and more expert at talking to customers with a standard set of chat up lines I began to hook around 50 per cent of customers using these techniques who would otherwise most probably of walked on down the street.

Large groups were another big target and the offer of three or four bottles of free wine always proved to be a winner. Remember one bottle of Rioja cost around 1 euro. Ten lads equals around 200 euros in the till.

It was just a job to me now, no big deal and I was bloody good at it.

This technique worked like a dream and one night I managed to pull in around a dozen young lads from Scotland who obviously liked a drink with the offer of three free bottles of wine.

Like with every large group there were a couple of guys in charge called Jim and Tony, who tended to make sure their mates kept out of any trouble and took on the role of group organisers.

On their second visit one or two of the Scottish lads were becoming a little loud and I nodded towards Jim to ask them to keep the noise down a bit. Jim had a quick word and the noise levels dropped immediately.

Suddenly without warning later in the night three local police burst through the doors of the restaurant carrying guns which caused the noise level to drop to zero as the shocked customers started to look a little worried.

'Has visto, negro?' the leading cop shouted a couple of times…'have you seen a coloured chap?'.

'No', I replied shaking my head.

The cops spread out in the restaurant checking everyone who was there and moved towards the back towards the two toilets and storerooms.

One of the cops checked the storerooms and the ladies toilets. The door of the male toilet was being used and locked.

They began to hammer on the door shouting for whoever was inside to come out.

It was one of the Scottish guys in the loo, naturally the one who had been making a lot of noise earlier in the evening and who was fairly drunk.

He started to swear from inside in a very strong Glaswegian accent.

'Fuck off...leave me alone you basas....', he slurred, thinking that it was his mates winding him up.

Jim realising that it was his mate who was in the toilet rushed to the door shouting.

'Kenny, Kenny it's the cops ...they've got their bloody guns out. Get out of there now!'

Kenny replied as before, 'Yes, Yes I believe you. Piss off you basa and leave me in peace'.

The cops were now becoming a little agitated and I thought that they were about to break down the door.

I shouted at Kenny,' Kenny, Jim's not kidding, there are cops outside. You have to come out of there now'.

There was a click as Kenny unlocked the door to be greeted by three police holding guns.

The colour on his face drained as he realised this was not a joke. He sobered up in seconds as he apologised to the cops and skulked off back to his seat. The cops walked out of the restaurant to continue their hunt leaving Kenny to receive abuse from his mates which I guess went on for some months to come.

The memorable night finished on a real high when it became apparent that one of the lads had gone missing.

'Where the hell is Jamie?' said Jim to the group looking very concerned.

'Went out to buy some fags', replied one of the group. 'Been gone for a while now'.

Aware of the regular muggings and of the amount of drink most probably consumed by Jamie I walked towards the door looking down the street.

Sat on a table at the Indian restaurant opposite was a young chap surrounded by four of the Chinese girls selling an array of toys with flashing coloured lights and an assortment of similar tat.

Jamie was festooned from head to foot looking like a demented Christmas tree, handing over wads of cash to the girls who were obviously encouraging him with great gusto.

Jim grabbed Jamie's arm and started to drag him down the street towards the other guys who had headed to the nearest bar about fifty metres from the Dom Miguel.

The young Chinese girls followed closely behind hoping that the other Scottish guys could also help them make their fortunes.

Business in September continued at a pace as the early British eaters meant I could turn each table a couple of times during the evening still pulling customers through the door with my well honed chat up lines.

If the restaurant was starting to empty we slowed down the service to keep the numbers looking reasonable to attract new customers. Once we began to fill again the service speeded up again. I was now starting to make a healthy profit smashing the 1,000 euro figure most nights.

One event during September finally made me realise that I wanted to leave Spain for good.

On a regular trip to the bank I asked for a statement for the last three months. The statement was around six pages long full mainly of details of each separate credit card payment which I left in the account to pay for my service charges and monthly rent.

Sitting down for a coffee later that day I pulled out the statement and began to check each item. Among the credit card takings and service charges for electric, phone, water etc I noticed around sixteen debits of around 5,000 euros in total, around six per month which I did not understand.

The next day I went back to the bank to see Christina to find out who these payments were being made to.

'Británico Associates', said Christina, 'Your solicitors'.

'What all of them?' I replied, 'I will have to take this to Carlos tomorrow to find out what they are for. I didn't know I had any direct debits set up for them'.

'In the meantime can you cancel the direct debit. I will pay them in future when they give me an invoice including a description of what I am supposed to be paying for', I continued.

The next day I dropped the statement off with Carlos highlighting the payments made to his firm.

A few days later I arrived at the abogados office to see Carlos with my box of invoices for him to complete my tax returns for the last three months.

'Did you look at the payments I sent you?' I said to Carlos.

'Yes', replied Carlos, and he started to go through each one.

'Ok', started Carlos, 'This is for me for accounts, next is for the NIE's ,next for Power of Attorney, this one for Boxto contract, this for service set up etc etc'.

'Ok, that makes sense', 'What about these?', I said pointing to five payments which he hadn't covered totalling around 1100 euros.

'Not sure', he said, 'Will have to check later', said Carlos.

The next week I went back to the bank again for a statement knowing that the payment for Carlos had been due to be taken from my account two days before.

I looked at the new statement and there it was, a payment for 100 euros had been taken out of my account.

I asked to see Christina who was in her office towards the back of the bank.

'Hi Christina', I said, 'I thought you had stopped the direct debit for Británico Associates'.

'I did', she replied as I showed her the payment on the statement. 'Let me check'.

She logged onto the desktop in front of her and began checking my account.

'There are three separate direct debits set up from Británico', said Christina.

'Three', I replied, 'Why three?'

'I do not know', she replied,' You must have agreed them when you signed the contract'.

'First I've heard of it', I replied, 'Look can you cancel them all before I go'.

'OK, one second', she said, as she cancelled each of the direct debits online.

I never did find out what those additional payments, the 1100 euros from Británico Associates were supposed to be for but my very low level of trust in dealing with the Spanish to start with had now fallen to minus fifty.

First suppliers and customers, next the bent cops, now my solicitor. Is there anyone I can trust in this bloody place?

From that day until I left Spain I only ever received a request for two additional payments from Carlos. They must have modelled their admin processes on the Spanish Tax system.

During September the great business being done in the Dom Miguel was being eroded by the problems in Boxto. Ross was doing his bit on the PR side attracting the Brits but the big Friday and Saturday nights of filling the place with Spanish were long gone.

September's rent was well short for Boxto and I was using profits made in the restaurant to make up the shortfall.

Time for another chat with Steve to see what could be done.

'Dad', said Steve, 'I've got two ideas we can try'.

'Go on then, let's hear them', I replied.

'One of the girls does Ann Summers parties. We could do one in Boxto'.

'Why not', I replied.' Try anything once'.

'Great, but I will need to set up Boxto with rows of seats for people to sit to see the stuff demoed. Can I borrow your chairs from the restaurant on Monday on your night off. We can borrow Bill's transit van from the port to ship them to Boxto'.

'OK, what's the other idea?' I said.

'Strippers', replied Steve, 'Had a guy in the other day offering them for 150 euros for 1 hour shows.

'Go on then, sort it out', I replied.

'Can you lend me the 150 euros? Pay you back later', said Steve.

I handed over the 150 euros knowing full well that I would never see this money again.

The following Monday we wandered down to the port to borrow Bills van to take the chairs from the restaurant to Boxto ready for the evenings Ann Summers party.

The event was a reasonable success in terms of numbers attending but the sale of drinks which was the main objective was not great. Anyway at least we tried, I thought to myself.

The real fun for me of the whole event was when we shipped the chairs back to the Dom Miguel in the van.

To do this we had to drive down a narrow one way street to park up about thirty metres from the restaurant to unload the chairs, around sixty of them from the van.

As we stopped on the road to unload with no traffic behind us, myself and Steve began to quickly unload the chairs onto the pavement ready to put back in the restaurant.

After we had done around half of the unloading in less than five minutes a car pulled up behind us who we were blocking in.

I waved to the driver who was a young Spanish girl raising a couple of fingers to say we would be only two minutes more to finish unloading the van.

Rather than just accepting this minor inconvenience the young lady started to shout at us through the window waving her arms around and repeating over and over, 'Policia, policia'.

I went over to her and said, 'Dos minutos, gracias..two minutes'.

This seemed to wind her up even more as she continued her rant with phone in hand looking as if she was calling the police.

'Right', I said to Steve who was next to me in the back of the van.' Let's sit down and make the bugger wait'.

Steve who thought this was amusing sat down next to me in the back of the van on two chairs as we both stopped the unloading process and placed both hands on our chins looking directly at the young lady.

After a few minutes of amusing ourselves doing this and the young girl now close to complete meltdown we slowly got back up and even more slowly continued to unload the chairs until we were done and ready to move on. Childish I know but quite enjoyed that.

The night of the stripper was a bit of a nightmare however. She was due at 12 midnight on the Thursday for her performance at Boxto and Steve, Ross and his mates had been advertising the fact around the main promenade for a 10 euro entrance fee. I even mentioned it to Hamed who said he would be there to watch the show.

At around 12.30am after closing the restaurant I made my way up to Boxto to see how it was going.

Halfway there I met Ross and Steve on the front.

'How are we doing?' I said.

'She's in the bar now having a few drinks but there is no one else in there', said Steve, 'She says she will stay till 1 and we are still trying to get people to come in'. Steve looked incredibly stressed.

'Ok, good luck', I said as I turned around to go back to the apartment.

Apparently, the stripping didn't happen that night even though Steve and Ross managed to pull a few guys into Boxto, but she managed to do some sort of exotic dancing perched on top of one of the large speakers for her 150 euros. Not a great success.

I normally spent my day off catching up on admin and cleaning the apartment and often went out with Steve for a meal to catch up on what he was up to.

We always started at big Ron's Pig and Parrot for a quick pint and game of pool before moving on to eat.

This night however the 'Pig' was quite busy and we ended up having three pints of big Ron's special brew. Now I expect you have heard the joke from comedians like Billy Connolly that after drinking certain special brews your legs cease to function.

Drinking big Ron's concoction which he sells at two euros a pint takes this to a new level. Remember as I said earlier this stuff was dynamite.

I remember walking out of the door down three steps when my legs gave way completely as I stumbled on to the pavement. Steve obviously thought this was hilarious as he was still just about managing to walk in a straight line.

'Let's go to Boxto before we go for a meal. There's a few club owners who want to meet you', said Steve.

I followed Steve carefully through the streets to Boxto to meet his mates who were sitting at a table outside of Boxto which was closed.

Steve quickly opened the bar and came outside with a bottle of Jack Daniels and four glasses and introduced me to the two bar owners.

'This is Mike and Roger. They own the clubs at the back of Boxto. Mike used to be a professional tennis player'.

Now I wasn't even aware that there was anything at all behind Boxto just two clubs either side.

'Hi, how's business?' I said.

'Enough to pay for my tennis. That's all I want', said Mike quickly finishing off his half full glass of Jack Daniels with me trying to keep up.

Steve refilled the glasses a few more times until Mike said. 'Right have to go now, we will be open. I need to check everything is OK....come with me for a quick drink at my place'.

It was now about 11pm and we still had managed not to eat a thing and I was becoming quite drunk.

Myself and Steve followed Mike through an alleyway leading to his club behind Boxto.

The place was alive with young people. Groups of girls were drinking god knows what with straws out of what looked like shared plastic buckets.

A heavy mist smelling of cannabis hung in the air and an array of coloured lights were flashing across the whole area making a surreal picture in front of me,

Guys obviously out of their minds on drugs were dancing and prancing around completely in a world of their own across the enclosed outside terrace area.

Mike came up to me and Steve holding another glass full of Jack Daniels which by this time was the last thing I needed.

The three of us were chatting leaning against an outside table when suddenly running towards me shouting and screaming and waving his arms around was what looked like a complete madman coming my way. He had a thick long, black beard, straggly hair and was just wearing some scruffy shorts with no shirt. He looked like a bloody caveman.

'Mike', I shouted pointing towards the lunatic running towards me.

Mike calmly took the drink out of my hand which I hadn't touched and stood up in front of this lunatic who stopped when he was about two metres in front of me. The mad guy stopped in his tracks for a second, tipped the half glass of Jack Daniel's down his throat, turned around and ran off again back to where he had come from still shouting and waving his arms around.

'Who the fuck was that?' I said.

'Regular', said Mike laughing.

We said goodbye to Mike and walked down an alley, this time to hit Rogers bar. At the end of the alley there was a very small bar and a large open area outside with a row of tables and chairs against a wall.

We squeezed into the small bar where Roger poured us two extra large measures of Jack Daniels with me feeling pleased that the mad Moroccan had finished off my other drink.

After about an hour we finished our drinks and walked outside the bar into the open area. It was now around 2am.

What I saw is something that will scar me forever.

On one table closest to the bar were sat three of four policemen just sat drinking. Behind them was a line of young Spanish lads around fifteen of sixteen years old all standing in a line up against the wall with their trousers or shorts around their ankles.

Kneeling in front of each of the boys were the black hookers who normally plied their trade on the front obviously doing their twenty euro tricks for the evening. People were sat on other tables completely oblivious to what was going on in front of them.

Steve looking at the expression on my face and laughing said, 'Time to go. I think...can you walk back OK or should I come with you?'

Still stunned I replied, 'Well the hookers won't be there to grab me on the front', and I set off back to the apartment really trying to concentrate on how to walk.

The next day was horrendous. I woke up still feeling quite drunk but still had my normal shopping, cleaning and other chores to do.

By about lunchtime the hangover started to kick in. This was not a normal hangover but a big Ron's special brew handover.

At 3pm I went back to the apartment where as usual Steve was still fast asleep. I spent the next hour draped over the toilet retching feeling close to death.

I managed to crawl into Steve's room, 'Can you run the restaurant tonight? I think I'm going to die', I muttered.

Steve jumped up and laughed. 'Yes, no problem. I feel fine'.

I returned to bed and slept through till 9pm that evening not really caring what was happening in the restaurant.

At 09.30pm I managed to drag myself up to the restaurant to see what was going on. The restaurant was half full.

'How's it going?' I said.

'Good. You look like shit get off home you will put off the customers', replied Steve.

I was again feeling close to throwing up again and turned towards the door and back to the apartment.

I never did sample more than two pints of big Ron's brew again from that day on.

Towards the end of September Steve's mates who were helping in Boxto started to return to the UK as the summer was coming to an end. I had had a couple of timewasters looking at buying Boxto but no definite offers to date.

One afternoon Steve arrived at the restaurant.

'I've found someone who wants to run Boxto', he said.

'What, buy it?' I replied

'Maybe, but he doesn't have the cash right now. He's called Roberto and he says he actually owned Boxto a few years ago when it was buzzing with the Spanish', continued Steve. 'Do you want to meet him?'

'Yes, why not', I replied. 'Can he meet me here tomorrow at 10am'.

The next day Roberto arrived as I was trying to get one of the ceiling lights in the restaurant to work. He was a fairly mature looking guy of around forty five years of age dressed in denim from head to foot. Roberto was of Dutch origin but had lived in Spain for the last twenty years.

'Having problems?' said Roberto.

'Yes, I can't get this bloody light to work. I've changed the bulb'.

'Let me try', said Roberto who quickly jumped up onto a chair to inspect the faulty light.

'Where is the switch?' he said.

'Behind the bar', I replied pointing to an array of around a dozen different switches each with labels showing what they were for.

Roberto grabbed a screwdriver sitting on top of the fuse box and started to strip back one of the switches and inspect the wiring.

After five minutes he turned and said, 'All fixed, just the wiring' and the light came back to life.

'Thanks', I said, 'I take it that you are Roberto'.

'Hi, yes I am Roberto I can also make Boxto work for you', he said.' We need to strip the whole place back and resurrect the old Boxto. Only I can do this, no one else'.

'Steve has no chance of making Boxto work. I have lived here twenty years and am Dutch not Spanish. The Spanish will not go to any English bar. The young Spanish do not like the English', continued Roberto.

He continued his pitch for a good twenty minutes without taking a breath.

'Do you want to buy it?' I said when I could get a word in.

'Yes', he replied. 'But we need to make some arrangements till I can afford it'.

'What arrangements?' I replied.

'I will look after Boxto, pay the rent and all the bills. Any profits will be 70% for me and 30% for you. I will do everything, said Roberto confidently. I will work with Steve and show him all I know'.

'Let me think about it', I replied. 'Come and see me again tomorrow and I will let you know'.

Roberto left the restaurant leaving me and Steve alone.

'What do you think?' I said to Steve.

Steve looked quite upset but resigned to the fact that we really had no choice and with the winter coming we would struggle to make Boxto remotely break even. Also he would be alone as his mates would all have gone home.

'We have no choice', said Steve. 'But I do not want to work there for him'.

'Will you work in the restaurant?' I said. 'Adar, the Finnish waiter in the restaurant is looking to go back home anyway'.

'Only if you pay me what you pay Hamed', replied Steve.

'Ok, it's a deal. Let me speak to Antonio the abogado. I think I will need to draw up a formal contract with Roberto'.

I rang Antonio that afternoon and he agreed that this looked like the best option for me. He would have the contract ready by the following Tuesday.

Roberto arrived back at the restaurant the next day and we shook hands on the deal.

'Right, we start now', he said. 'Let me have the keys'.

'I will be working with Manuel, who helped me before to run Boxto. First we need to rebuild the old Boxto'.

The next day I walked up to Boxto with Steve to see what was happening.

The place was like a building site. All of the old signs had been removed and the original ones reinstated and the bar floor was being sanded down by Manuel. The speaker systems were in bits on the terrace with Roberto busily trying to rebuild the original sound system. The rubbish that had accumulated in a store at the back of the bar was also stacked up outside.

'Phil', he shouted over.' I need a lift ..now. I need parts for the speakers'.

'Ok, ten minutes', I will get the car'.

In the car I mentioned that we had two young girls who could work for him behind the bar.

'No girls', he said. 'Big mistake, you need handsome boys'.

'Why?' I replied, 'I would have thought that the girls behind the bar would attract the guys into the bar'.

'No, no', he replied. 'Good looking boys behind the bar attract the girls, then the girls attract more boys. That is how it works', said Roberto.

'You also need to get rid of the one litre bottles of spirits', he said. 'Spanish only drink out of 70 cl bottles. They believe all litre bottles are fake'.

'Eddies spirits fake, perish the thought', I thought to myself.

Soon we were off into the town to a back street shop selling sound systems and speaker parts to find the missing bits.

We returned to the bar. 'Come back in two days, I want to show you the old Boxto', said Roberto.

'OK, I'll leave you in peace', I replied feeling that maybe I had made a good decision.

Two days later I returned to Boxto. The place was immaculate.

'Come, let me show you', said Roberto as he walked towards the DJ plinth.

'You stand there', he said pointing to the corner of the bar.

Roberto played some music which had a fantastic tone from the newly rebuilt speaker system.

'Now walk to each corner and listen', said Roberto.

The distinctive sounds from each of the different speakers sounded great.

'What do you think, better eh?' said Roberto.

I was very impressed.

'We will open on Friday, I just need to finish this other bar'.

Roberto pointed to the far corner of Boxto which was in the process of having a new separate bar built.

'We will sell more with two bars', he said.

'What about money for the drinks?' I said.

'No worries' he replied, 'I will get drinks on credit from San Miguel. I do not need any money for this'.

I left the bar feeling very optimistic that maybe, just maybe Roberto could turn the place around. Without question he was a hard worker. Now I could forget about Boxto and concentrate fully on making the restaurant work.

Steve was now working in the restaurant and was a great asset and especially good at pulling in new customers.

Things were going great now until one night I received a call from my sister Barbara saying that my dad was in hospital and things were not looking good.

I immediately made plans to fly back to the UK leaving Steve to run the restaurant confident he would do a good job as long as I had stocked up on the food and drink.

I left the next day to fly back to Manchester airport and after picking up my wife and son David, drove the 170 miles up to the North East to see my dad.

Walking into the hospital ward I could see him lying on a bed in the corner. He was unrecognisable from the last time I saw him less than one year before and any conversation with him was very difficult.

We left the ward early as he said he was tired and he wanted us to leave and as I walked to the car we all knew that this was the last time we would see him alive. No one really spoke as we drove back to the north west.

I was back in Fuengirola the day I was due to sign the new contract with Roberto and we both sat down with Antonio, the abogado in his office.

Antonio again was confident that this was the sensible move to make for me as we both duly signed the new papers.

As myself and Roberto left the office I sat down for a quick coffee with Roberto and pulled out the statement of accounts for the previous year I had received from the previous owners demonstrating the profitability of Boxto.

Roberto glanced at the papers.

'Rodrigo's a crook', said Roberto, 'I know him well'. These papers are rubbish', he continued. 'I know what the business did last year'.

'Antonio has seen them. I assumed they were legit', I replied

'Antonio and Rodrigo are friends', said Roberto shaking his head.

'Shit', I said, 'I should have used a different abogado, shouldn't I?'

Roberto nodded and handed me back the papers. I felt sick at what he had just told me.

I mentioned the direct debit fiasco to Roberto.

'You will learn', replied Roberto as we both got up to leave.

The next week I visited Boxto late one night to check on the progress of his opening week. There were a few quite well dressed and older Spanish drinking and chatting by the bar. The quality of the clientele had definitely improved. Music was blaring out as usual and Roberto was sat in the corner taking charge of a newly installed laptop managing the order of the record plays.

I wandered over to Roberto who was engrossed in his work.

'How's it going?' I enquired.

'Early yet, we need to get the word out that we are back' he replied. 'I had to get rid of my friend Manuel, he has become very lazy. Not my friend any more'.

I went to the bar for a drink and sat on the terrace of Boxto close to the bouncer who seemed to be turning most people away.

'Why are you not letting them come in?' I asked the bouncer

'We only want customers with money to spend', he replied.

I finished my drink and left thinking that Roberto obviously knew what he was doing.

During mid October Barbara arrived for a few days with two friends who she worked with in the UK. She was pleasantly surprised to see how well the restaurant was now doing and even more surprised to see how much I had changed especially in pulling customers into the restaurant which I was now expert at.

I obviously took the opportunity of sticking Barbara and her two friends on a table next to one of the menus outside to chat up potential customers in return for a free meal.

She was also much happier that Steve was now working in the restaurant and away from the perils of Boxto.

I was now opening seven days a week to take advantage of the trade and the extra income and tips for Hamed and the crew was going down very well. With Steve able to run the service if not the logistics of shopping and cleaning I was able to have a couple of nights off each week which definitely pleased Steve especially that I was out of the way. Although I always made sure I was there from six till eight to pull the customers through the door to reach the quarter full target.

Barbara left after a few days with a bag full of euros from the profits we had made to take back to the UK through customs, although the local Barclays in the UK was not used to customers arriving with bundles of foreign banknotes over the counter to put into their accounts. I think that these days you may be challenged about money laundering and she was very relieved when she left the bank without any questions being asked.

It was now the last day in October at around 7pm when I got the news I had been expecting but dreading. A call from my sister Barbara that my dad had passed away earlier that evening.

The restaurant was quite busy at the time with about twenty or so customers. I was obviously overcome with the news and desperately trying to make my brain work to figure out what to do. Should I close the restaurant. I would have to tell Steve who was due to arrive for his shift in the next half hour or should I wait till the end of the evening.

I told Hamed, Halima and Carin the news and told them not to say anything to Steve until we had finished that night.

After about half an hour I knew I had made the wrong decision as overcome with grief I had to walk out of the restaurant away from the customers into the street. Barry and Karen were walking towards me up the street and obviously could see something was wrong.

I was stood facing a wall in floods of tears being comforted by Karen who told me that she would help that night.

Some of Steve's mates walked by looking across in puzzlement at what was going on. They could see something was wrong, but continued walking.

Eventually, I calmed down a little and told Karen that I would be able to just get through tonight OK by myself. She offered to run the restaurant for me for the next few days while I went back to the UK to help with any arrangements and said she would come back at closing time for a quick briefing before I left the next day.

Steve arrived at the restaurant and knew something was wrong. He had met some of his mates on the way there and they had obviously told him about what they had seen in the street.

'I'll tell you later', I said and continued the best I could to get through the most painful night I had ever had.

At the end of the evening as the staff were leaving Steve came up to me and said, 'It's grandad isn't it?'

'Yes', I replied in tears. 'We have to go back tomorrow, early'.

Steve just turned and went out of the restaurant obviously trying to take in what he had just been told.

Karen arrived a short time later and as best I could I took her through the till and other bits and pieces so that she could manage the restaurant while I was away. I also rang Hamed to ask if he would look after the shopping for a few days and would leave 1,000 euros in the till to which he readily agreed.

I went out looking for Steve that night and walked miles to find him without any success. We had to arrange the flights.

The next day I had arranged to fly back with Steve at three o'clock so managed to do some quick shopping before I left before I handed over the keys to Karen.

Finishing the shopping in record time I returned to the restaurant and could not believe what was waiting for me.

The restaurant floor was a complete mess. Soggy lasagne covered the bar, the floor and three or four tables. Drink was spilled all over the floor and the tablecloths were sodden with beer.

In the kitchen the microwave door was open with the inside covered in more lasagne sticking to the top and sides and across all of the work surfaces.

It looked as if a bomb had hit the place and it really was the last thing I needed in the current situation.

I began cleaning up the mess becoming more and more angry.

After an hour I had the place reasonably respectable as Karen arrived at the door, took control and told me to go and not worry.

I marched back to the apartment where Steve as usual was asleep and the stress and pain of the last few hours caught up with me.

I marched into Steve's bedroom.

'Right, get up and get out of here, now. What the hell do you think you are doing? Your grandad's just died. Do you think I have got time to clean up your bloody mess as well at a time like this. I have enough to do. You thoughtless little bugger'.

Steve knowing that nothing he could say would have been remotely acceptable immediately jumped out of bed, and was out of the door in seconds. I never saw him again that day.

I spent the next hour packing a bag and wandering up the promenade looking for Steve to no avail. At 1pm I headed for the train to take me to the airport for the 3 o'clock flight back to the UK.

Arriving home at around 07.30pm I opened the door to see Steve sat with his mum and brother David looking sheepish.

'You're here are you', I said, quite relieved actually to see him sat there.

'Sorry dad, I just felt like shit and didn't realise what I was doing'.

I spent the rest of the evening explaining to Barbara what had happened over the last few hours. To this day she could never understand how I managed to work through that night.

After the funeral I returned on my own to Spain. Steve had had enough and decided to look for a job in the UK and anyway I was looking to sell up.

The restaurant was still standing and I paid Karen for her time. The takings for the three days away had been poor and I even received a compliment from Hamed about how they had missed my expertise at dragging in customers.

As it was now November I decided that Carin and I could easily manage the service as the terrace was to all intents and purposes not being used as the weather started to cool.

Winter Approaches

I continued to follow my regular routine timed to the minute but on three out of the next five days I had trouble with my car....and the local plod.

It was always the most stressful part of the day when I had to park up on the pavement outside the cafe in the street to unload the car. Once parked and quickly looking around for signs of the police I would dash into the restaurant, grab the trolley and run backwards and
forwards between the car and restaurant with three trolley loads of food, literally throwing the food on the restaurant floor ready to clear away later. The whole process took around five minutes before I was ready to drive away and park legally about one kilometre up the road.

On the first day as I had just dumped the first trolley load of food on the restaurant floor standing by the car were two Spanish police posing in their designer shades.

'Restaurante, carretilla...restaurant trolley', I shouted smiling of course.

'No estacionar...no parking', replied one of the policemen.

'Si,si', I said 'I will go now', as I went to get into the driver's side of the car.

'No, No', said the more miserable cop who stopped me from entering the car.

''I need to get the food out', I said to the grumpy looking cop.

'No, No', he said.

I then gave up trying to speak Spanish and broke into my more natural tongue.

'For fucks sake take the bloody car if you have nothing better to do, but let me get the food out'.

This actually seemed to work as the less miserable cop nodded for me to put the rest of the food in the trolley.

By now the usual crowd of onlookers sitting in the cafe were being highly amused by this sideshow and some of the English lads were shouting 'Leave him alone, bloody cops you are all the same'.

The cops now were even less amused and in a few seconds a tow truck had arrived to load my car and take it off to the pound.

They were greeted by a chorus of boos from the crowd as the cop handed me a ticket as my car moved off behind the tow truck.

I was familiar with the routine now and headed first to the local police station to pay my fine and then jumped into a taxi to take me to the car pound which relieved me of another 80 euros.

When I had finished with my car for the day I always drove along the coast road for around half a mile to park it on one of three roads on a local housing estate. It was often difficult to find a parking spot and often I had to drive a little further where I could park it outside a row of shops which had a large waste area to the side.

On this particular day as usual I went to collect the car from the waste ground and it was not where I thought I had parked it. Now that may sound a little unusual but as I had to park the car in a different place each day it was not unusual for me to spend 10 minutes trawling the streets looking for it. There was no trace of my car and I began to become a little worried as I thought it had been stolen.

I walked up to the police station to see if they knew anything and was greeted by the same clerk as I had dealt with a couple of days before.

'Not you again', she said.

'My car's been stolen', I said, and gave her the registration number.

'We've got it, it's in the pound, usual place', replied the clerk smiling.

'Why, I always park around there?' I said.

'Ah, every month on a Saturday the waste ground is used for a market, no cars allowed', said the clerk. 'All cars are towed away'.

To be honest I felt quite relieved that the car had not been stolen and handed over the fine before traipsing off again to the pound to pay the rest of the fine and retrieve my car.

On the following day as usual I walked up to find the car this time absolutely sure where I had parked it the day before to find glass from the driver's side window on the ground and covering the front seat.

'Not again', I thought. It was the only car with British number plates parked along the residential streets.

'Spanish bastards', I muttered to myself.

I found the first aid box on the floor of the car with its contents scattered around it.

'Hope he chopped his bloody finger off', I said to myself.

Fortunately there was a Peugeot dealership not far from Lidl which I passed everyday so after my normal shopping trip I drove into the forecourt of the dealer and walked up to the service desk.

The service chap followed me outside to inspect the damage.

'Yes, we can fix that for you but I will need to see your registration document', he said.

'I don't have it over here. It's in the UK', I replied.

'I have to see it', replied the chap.

'Ok, I will have it mailed to me to show you, but would you please fix the window', I said.

'Wait here', said the chap, 'I need to speak to the boss'.

Soon he returned. 'OK we fix the window tomorrow for you no problem, but next time make sure you bring your documents'.

'No problem', I replied. The next day the window was replaced. Now the saying that things always happen in threes is true. Two parking fines and a replacement window in five days. My bad luck must be now over.

November in the restaurant was quite healthy in terms of takings which although running around the thirty to forty covers a night figure were helped by the price increases I had introduced. I also had a consistent number of locals who had become good friends coming into the restaurant.

One particular incident during late November sticks in my mind because it was the one and only time that I had ever had any semblance of trouble with British customers.

It was a reasonably busy night when two British chaps around thirty years of age came into the restaurant at around 10pm. They had obviously had a few drinks and didn't appear to be over friendly with Carin who took their order for paella.

It was obvious from their manner that they had fallen out with each other and they sat together in silence picking at the large dish of paella in front of them.

As usual at the end of the meal Carin took over the bill for around 30 euros and left it on the table sat on a small silver tray which we used for customers to leave their cash.

The guys left their cash in the tray and wandered out of the restaurant.

Carin picked up the tray and shouted across to the bar.

'Phil, there is just 10 euros here', she said.

I immediately dashed from behind the bar running outside of the door and up the street looking for the two guys.

I found them about 50 metres up the road.

'You owe me 20 euros', I said. 'There are only 10 here'.

'Piss off', the smaller chap replied. 'The food was shit, that's all you are getting'.

I knew at this point that continuing the conversation would be pointless as they looked to be up for trouble so I turned around and headed back to the restaurant.

The next day after shopping and cleaning the restaurant I headed about 100 metres up the street to an English cafe/bar called the Yorkshire Rose that I frequented occasionally for a bacon sandwich with real English bacon. I knew the owners quite well as they had been to the Dom Miguel a couple of times on their nights off.

As I walked inside the restaurant one of the chaps who had not paid my bill the night before was sat on his own having breakfast.

I sat down behind him at a table with him facing away from me.

Catherine, one of the staff who I knew quite well and actually came to work for me in the Dom Miguel in the following year came to my table to take my order.

I placed my usual order and said in a loud voice.

'I would make sure that this guy pays up front before you give him any food', knowing the chap could hear me clearly.

'Yes, he was in my restaurant last night and walked out without paying the bill'.

The chap in front turned round to face us obviously embarrassed..

'Oh, er, er I was here looking for you. I couldn't remember which restaurant we were in last night', said the chap looking very sheepish.

'How much do I owe you?' he continued.

'20 euros', I replied.

The chap pulled out 25 euros from his wallet and handed the missing cash to me.

'Thanks', I said as he got up and walked out before his meal arrived at the cafe. Great result.

During the final week of November four elderly chaps from Northern Ireland came into the Dom Miguel at around 11pm and sat at the table directly in front of the bar.

As usual I took the menus to the table when one of the chaps called Liam said that they just wanted drinks, no food.

''How much for a bottle of Jamesons whisky', said Liam.

This caught me by surprise and I mumbled, 'Is 30 euros OK? I don't normally sell by the bottle'.

'40 and we have a deal', the chap said smiling. 'That seems fairer to me'.

'Great', I replied, and went to open the fresh bottle of Jamesons and bring four glasses to the table.

The guys sat and chatted for a while and ordered a second bottle of Jameson's and four beers. The restaurant was now empty as Hamed had gone home and I was stood behind the bar, just hoping that they would leave soon and let me close up.

I couldn't help but hear their conversation from around five feet away as I was washing the glasses and the volume of their conversation increased a few notches.

In very broad Irish brogue I could clearly hear a number of phrases which began to worry me.

'Should have kneecapped that fucker when we had the chance'.

'His son needs sorting out next. Getting too big for his boots. Just like the old man'.

'He will pay for that the bastard, Sean is on the case'.

It was now 2am and by this time I had moved to stand by the door not wanting to hear anything that was being said and that I may regret.

Karen and Barry walked past and I explained what was going on and pleaded with them to come in for a quick drink, but mainly so that I was not on my own with these chaps.

The three of us stood at the far end of the bar well away from the four Irish chaps making nervous conversation about nothing in particular.

Finally at 02.30am Liam threw 150 euros onto the bar and left with his three mates.

'Cheers, thanks for putting up with us', said Liam as they trudged out of the restaurant.

'Thank god for that', I said to Karen and Barry

'Can we go home now?' said Barry laughing.

'Yes, I owe you one', I replied, and off they went with me closing the bar in record time in case the four chaps returned.

On the last day of November I rang Roberto to discuss the accounts for the two months he had been running Boxto.

We met at a local cafe and he sat down with a scruffy piece of paper in front of him covered in a random number of scribbled words in Spanish. I obviously could not make head nor tail of what was written down.

Roberto who could talk for England then went into an incomprehensible babble of utter rubbish trying to explain how he was struggling to make ends meet.

'No people, low wages, recession, euro pound exchange rates...'. I had heard these excuses many times from other bar owners who always seemed to be complaining.

'Look all I want to see is a sheet of paper with outgoings on the left and takings on the right', I said.' This doesn't mean a thing to me'.

He went on to explain how Boxto had been broken into a couple of weeks before and the till had been stolen as well as lots of spirits, in the usual Spanish way of throwing his arms around to stress how difficult life had been for him. Like I said before he had been in Spain over twenty years and their standard mannerisms had obviously rubbed off on him.

'Ok', I said. 'Next month I want to see some figures', although I could see he was not really listening.

I left Roberto a little annoyed that he could not show me any accounts but comforted by the fact that I hadn't had to pay any rent or service charges for the last two months. By this point to be honest I was thinking about Boxto less and less each day and just concentrating on the Dom Miguel.

December had now arrived and business nosedived in the restaurant as the tourists disappeared. The terraces of all the restaurants in the area were now out of action although I still had to set up the terrace as usual just to move the extra tables and chairs outside. The toldo outside was opened up completely to cover the terrace area and the heating was switched on inside the restaurant for the first time.

I did a regular recce up and down the strip to see how the other restaurants were doing. It was very quiet everywhere. Carin had now left the restaurant and I employed a young British girl called Hannah to take over. Many nights Hannah would just work for a few hours often starting at 7pm and leaving at 10. The worst night I remember we had two customers through the door although we still averaged around fifteen to twenty covers during the first two weeks of December which was better than most of my competitors. But the nights were very long.

One thing that kept me going was the knowledge that I would be receiving a huge bonus from San Miguel on the 14th December. Every year at this time Sam Miguel doled out 20% cashback on all orders placed during the year and as I was spending well over 100 euros a week I had calculated I would be handed around 1,200 euros which would be a great help during this quiet period.

The way San Miguel operated was that a chap called Jose would arrive every Monday to take any orders for the following Thursday which was delivery day. Every Thursday I left the empty barrels of draught outside the restaurant which were replaced with new ones.

Jose arrived as usual on the Monday to take my order and I checked with him that the cash would be coming the following week.

The next week Jose arrived to take my order as usual.

'Where is the cash?' I enquired after giving him my order.

'No cash', he replied, 'My boss says that you must pay for toldo'.

'What toldo?' I asked thinking to myself here we fucking go again.

'Sam Miguel paid for your toldo outside. You must pay back', he continued.

'Bollox', I replied. 'The toldo came with the restaurant. Get the money from George, the previous owners. Nothing to do with me'.

'No', replied Jose, 'My boss says you pay'.

I was starting to become angry now.

'Well go and get your bloody boss down here now and show me where I have agreed to pay for his bloody toldo. And until you do you can cancel this order and don't bother coming back', I said.

'We will have to take toldo, if you don't order with us', continued Jose.

'Touch that toldo and I will personally stick this bottle of vodka up your arse. Now piss off'.

Jose walked to the door saying, 'Not my fault senor, I'll bring boss'.

'Yes, just do that, bring your bloody boss', I replied.

The next day still annoyed I had a chat with Carlos about the incident.

Carlos was on my side. 'When the boss comes let me speak to him', he said.

In the meantime I was selling only bottled beer, still buying San Miguel, but not from the main supplier. It was during this time that I noticed for the first time how much I had been drinking.

During a normal evening I always had half glass of draught San Miguel on the go which I filled up regularly as I passed to and fro by the pumps behind the bar.

With no draft now in the restaurant I had to open bottles to keep me topped up during the evening. When I reached into the fridge for my sixth bottle it hit me how much I had been drinking without even noticing. I just said to myself that it must be that which gave me the confidence to chat to strangers to persuade them into the restaurant. Worth every penny of the beer I concluded to myself.

Around two weeks later I was in the restaurant cleaning when the 'San Miguel boss', Mateus, arrived with Jose and I think he began to regret his opening comments before they had left his lips.

With a smug look on his face he said, 'We will also have to take out beer pumps and cooler as well as the toldo if you not order San Miguel with us'.

I erupted immediately. 'Look matey, you will not touch anything in this restaurant. Show me the agreement about the toldo. Where is it?'

At this point Mateus suddenly forgot how to speak or understand English looking at me with a blank expression. I was now absolutely beside myself with rage.

'Look you prick show me proof of supplying the toldo and proof that I have agreed to pay for it. I am sick and tired of being ripped off by bloody suppliers over here'. By this point I had completely lost it and didn't care what I was saying.

'Wait there', I said, 'I want you to speak to my abogado', and I picked up the phone for Carlos.

He wasn't available and I left an urgent message with Stella who definitely got the message that this was important.

The two San Miguel guys were huddled together chatting when after about five minutes the phone rang. It was Carlos.

I handed the phone to Mateus who began to have a fairly heated discussion with Carlos.

After a few minutes he put the phone down and from his inside pocket handed me an envelope containing the 1,200 euros.

It caught me totally by surprise as it was the last thing I was expecting and I didn't know how to react.

Jose piped up to interrupt the shocked silence, 'Is it two barrels for Thursday?'

'Eh, yes, thanks', I replied still in complete shock and the two guys left the restaurant with a quick 'Adios'. Bugger me I thought to myself as I wandered off to tell Barry and Karen the news.

The next episode involved Halima, Hamed's assistant. Her contract was now up and I needed to renew it within the next day or two.

Again, I used Carlos to take me to the employment office to renew her contract for me.

The following night after the new contract was signed Hamed came up to me at the end of service with Halima following behind.

'Halima is pregnant, she is asking for maternity leave from next week', he said.

'I just renewed her contract yesterday. Did she not know she was pregnant then?'

'Yes', replied Hamed.

I was thinking quickly through the consequences, feeling that once again I was being stitched up having to pay Halima as well as finding someone else to take over her job.

'We need to speak to Carlos to sort this out', I said to Hamed who repeated it to Halima in Spanish.

'Can we meet here at 10am tomorrow and I will drive us to see him to explain to me what I need to do from a legal point of view?'

Hamed translated again and Halima nodded back to me.

'Hasta manana', she said as she left....'See you tomorrow'.

The next day Halima arrived with two of her friends who I hadn't seen before for company and we all set off in the car to see Carlos in his office.

Myself, Halima and her two friends sat down in a private office with Carlos and immediately the four of them kicked off a conversation in Spanish which I did not understand.

Carlos turned to me. 'You need to pay four months maternity', he said.' You have signed the contract'.

'Shit', I thought to myself. 'Can I not just pay her off?' I replied.

'Yes', said Carlos, 'There is another way. It will cost you 160 euros'.

'Excellent', I replied. 'Let's do that then. Will I have to keep her job open?'

'No', said Carlos, that will be it.

Carlos then turned to the three of them and explained my decision to them to pay the 160 euros.

Halima and her two mates went into a huddle to ponder the outcome and spoke again to Carlos.

'She now wants to keep working', said Carlos. 'When it is too much her brother will cover for her'.

'Great perfect', I replied, quite relieved at the outcome.

We all left the office and the three of them headed off down the road not accepting the offer of my lift back. Another one sorted.

Christmas was now just over a week away and together with Hamed we produced a five course menu for Christmas day. In Fuengirola unlike the UK, Christmas meals are not on the menu during the whole of December just Christmas day itself. We prepared the menu, five courses for 25 euros adults and 12 euros for the kids with the standard fare of smoked salmon or soup, turkey roast, black forest gateau or Christmas pudding and finally cheese and biscuits and a coffee. Spainsburys along the road came into its own providing Paxo stuffing, Cranberry sauce and the Christmas Puddings.

Bookings for the big day came in steadily until I had taken deposit for around ten tables.

My wife Barbara had arrived on Christmas Eve and planned to stay until after the New Year, not that it was a holiday for her, as she would be expected to help in the restaurant obviously helping myself and Hannah.

Christmas day finally arrived and at around 6.30pm the first four customers sat down for their meal. Just as I was serving their drinks Hannah, my waitress arrived at the restaurant looking very Christmassy in her Santa hat with tinsel draped around her neck.

I asked her to take the order and pad in hand she walked across the restaurant floor towards the customers table knocking into a couple of chairs during her short journey.

I looked up from behind the bar and immediately realised she was completely drunk. I came quickly from behind the bar to take over from her but just too late as she crashed into the customer's table sprawling across the lap an oldish lady who was sat there looking bewildered.

Hannah stood up and without me saying a word she headed unsteadily for the door and out of the restaurant.

I immediately apologised to the two couples who thankfully found the whole episode quite amusing.

Within the next half hour the restaurant started to fill quickly. I was on my own as Barbara had still not arrived and was starting to worry.

I rang Barbara with no reply and dashed into the street to see if big Ron who lived above the Dom Miguel was around to see if his wife Molly could help for the evening, without success.

Back in the restaurant I was becoming more and more desperate trying to serve around six or seven tables on my own which was made doubly difficult as I had to serve a brand new Christmas menu as well as the normal one.

Finally, just after 07.30pm Barbara arrived and by this point I really was struggling to manage which must have been noticed by the customers who were expecting an enjoyable Christmas dinner.

'Where the hell have you been?' I said to Barbara as she came through the door.

'Why, what's up, where's Hannah?' she replied.

'Pissed', I said 'Will tell you later'.

'We're going to have to stop people coming in. The whole thing is out of control. I've no idea where the tables are up to or what their next orders are. Two tables are still waiting for drinks. I really can't cope with this', I said stood next to the bar with my head in my hands ready to just close the place.

'Stop being a wuss', she said.' Look I'll do the Christmas tables. I don't know either of the menus really so it makes no difference to me. You just do the other tables with the normal menu'.

'Right', I said and for the next three hours we were both flying around the restaurant like a couple of maniacs trying to restore some semblance of order in the place.

After a couple of hours I looked up for the first time to see that we really were going to pull it off and I could see the end in sight as some of the tables were now empty.

We had done it.

The next night Hannah came in as normal at around 6.

'I'm sacked aren't I', she said sheepishly.' It was my family's fault, they have come over to spend Christmas here and insisted I had a few drinks with them'.

'Correct, you are sacked', I replied. Yet another new waiter needed. Lost count now.

The next day indulging in my now regular bacon sandwich at the Yorkshire Rose I was telling Catherine the waitress about our Christmas day adventure which she thought was very amusing.

'Guess you need a waitress?' said Catherine.

'Yes, do you know anyone looking for a job', I replied.

''Yes, me, I could start tomorrow if you want. They are closing here for a couple of months', she continued.

'Great, see you tomorrow. Come in at five and I will take you through the table layout and the rest of the routine', I said.

Now New Year in Spain like the UK is really the big night out of the entire year. I had spoken at length to Hamed about what we should do and received three valuable pieces of advice.

'Take off the three daily menus, hike up the prices of the a la carte and reduce the choices', said Hamed.

I spent the run up to the New Year re printing the a la carte menu and adding several euros to each item ready for the big night.

I hired one extra experienced waitress who worked at the cafe on the front called Bahora who I knew quite well just for the New Year's evening service and asked Barbara to sit at the corner of the bar close to the restaurant entrance and just welcome all new customers, sitting them at the bar serving drinks while waiting for tables to become free.

New Years Eve went off like a dream. We were packed from 7pm until 12 with a steady stream of customers waiting by the bar waiting to be seated. It was the perfect night, all a la carte with hiked up prices and loads of wine and cava.

As customers left the restaurant it was obvious that the takings per head were double the norm. At the end of the service I counted the takings ....2500 euros for 1 night more than I was taking in 6 nights when I first arrived in April.

The New Year

After the highs of New Year's Eve the first few days up to around the 7th of January were reasonable as the locals and a few of the British here for the New Year's holidays continued their celebrations.

From the 8th of January it started to rain and rain some more. Every night was painful. There really was no one around until the end of January.

Takings were well down and I was struggling some nights to even break the 10 cover mark. Luckily I had some savings to cover this lack of business but the nights were long, cold and bloody wet.

I was stood at the door most nights in my jumper and coat gazing into the empty street, totally bored.

As usual every night I set up the tables outside inside the toldo really just for somewhere to put them as I couldn't accommodate them inside.

I didn't set cutlery on the outside tables as there was no point just a few ashtrays for the odd smoker who now had to go outside for a fag or two.

During this time I began to notice that on four consecutive nights an ash tray would disappear from the seven or eight tables outside. Now I always put the really quite expensive ceramic colourful ashtrays on the tables outside which looked quite attractive.

I made it my mission, due to complete boredom to find out where the ashtrays were mysteriously going.

The next night I watched from inside the door to catch the culprit and at around 9pm I noticed a hand appear through one of the side panels of the toldo reaching across the table.

I dashed to the table and made a grab for the hand. The culprit an oldish guy of around sixty years of age pulled his hand away and started running up the road with me shouting behind him.

Never lost anymore ashtrays after that.

I think that was the high point during late January for me. It was a really painful two weeks or so. Next year I would close the first two weeks in December and last two weeks in January if I am still here.

Thankfully January ended without much incident and I spent most of any free time in the local British bars with Dave in his bar 'Spanish Sunshine or with Karen or Barry who had now opened a new cafe bar called 'Little Britain' on the front playing pool. Staying in the apartment was not a great option for me as I had no TV, except for the Travel channel, and I was becoming fed up with trying to play the dodgy videos sold by the coloured chaps which usually did not reach the end of the film before they stopped working and it was really cold in the apartment.

I had also received notice from the Town Hall that the pedestrianised street outside the restaurant was due to be dug up and re-laid sometime in the next few months. This was a worry as I had noticed that a similar road further down the street had recently just completed the same treatment. It had taken around three months to complete and the businesses were greatly affected by the mess.

In February, British half term arrived and business was starting to pick up as the Brits looking for some early sunshine after the local winter in the UK started to arrive. Now with my new skills of attracting customers, which I had perfected from the previous year meant I was hitting the 35 to 40 cover target easily to break even

even this early in the year. For some unexplained reason there was always a really poor night during the week which I cannot explain at all, but I now had a solid base of locals and regulars who I could rely on.

On one particular evening a couple arrived, for a meal. I had served them drinks and they were busy looking through the menu when the chap waved me over.

'Hi, I'm Nick', said the chap, 'I see you've got creme caramel on the menu'.

'Yes', I replied, Do you want to order that for dessert? What about mains?'

'No', said Nick, 'Can I have that first?' which seemed very odd.

I went to the kitchen and asked Hamed to prepare the creme caramel which I took across to Nick.

He could see I was looking puzzled.

'Bet you think I am a bit strange', said Nick.

'It's the first time I've served dessert first', I replied.

'I wanted to test your food', he replied.' I am head chef at the Connaught Hotel in London and only once in my life I have been served creme caramel as it should be made with the right consistency and no bubbles. No bubbles is the key'.

'Oh', I replied, 'What do you think?'

'Best I have ever had, you have a great chef in there', said Nick.

I went immediately to tell Hamed who just raised his eyebrows in response.

The couple then ordered their mains from the a la carte menu.

Nick piped up, 'Do you do specials?'

'Yes', I replied and pointed to the three specials at the back of the menu.

'I would like lobster thermidor', said Nick,' Can your chef do it?'

'No idea', I replied. 'I'll go and get him'.

The restaurant was quite quiet at the time and Hamed came across and began chatting to Nick.

'Need to add to your shopping list tomorrow', said Hamed. He wants me to prepare lobster thermidor for tomorrow night'.

'No problem', I replied, 'But where the hell do I get lobster?'

'Eroski fish counter', replied Hamed.

The next night Nick and his partner arrived as promised for their meal and again were very complimentary towards Hamed's work apart from there being no lobster claws available.

'You're not having Hamed', I joked to Nick. 'I'm not sure what to charge you. I could charge you anything I want'. How about 200 quid based on what you probably charge in the Connaught?'

'Make it 100 euros for the two and we have a deal', said Nick.

'Sounds good to me, 100 it is', I replied.

On finishing their meal Nick popped into the kitchen to thank Hamed for the excellent meal and their conversation about food started all over again.

'Can you do Beef Wellington?' said Nick

'No problem', replied Hamed, who I think was very pleased at the opportunity to cook some other dishes for a change.

'OK, same time tomorrow', said Nick as he left the restaurant.

The next night Nick returned and again was very complimentary about the dish although he did offer some advice about how to improve the pastry to Hamed who seemed pleased at the feedback.

So everyone was happy with the results especially me with another 100 euro payment for the one off meal.

I did visit Roberto only on one occasion again during February to be fobbed off with a load of pre prepared hard luck stories as to why he had not made any profits. Again, I thought to myself at least responsibility for any bills were being covered so I did not make a big issue of this. After all, he did take control of Boxto after the main Spanish summer period and anyway I was making reasonable profits in the restaurant. Best to just wait it out I thought until I could sell the place.

One afternoon in February I came to clean the restaurant as usual to find the water supply had been cut off. Checking along the street the problem seemed to be only affecting four of the restaurants besides the Dom Miguel. Walking to the top of the street I noticed a gang of three Spanish workers beside a large hole at the side of the road.

I approached the three guys and in my best Spanish said, 'No Agua..restaurante'.

'Ok, dos horas', replied one of the chaps...'two hours'.

'Gracias', I replied, knowing that they would be finished well before Hamed arrived to start the prep for the evening.

I returned to the apartment to change and returned to the Dom Miguel just before 5pm.

The water in the restaurant was still off and I started walking up the street towards where the three guys had been working. They had disappeared, obviously finished for the day.

Panic began to set in as there was no way we could open without water to cook or wash up with or especially to flush the toilets.

I wandered into the local off license on the corner which I used most days to buy cigarettes and asked if they still had their water running.

The owner went to check returning to say, 'Si, agua OK, you use if you want'.

I returned to the restaurant where Hamed and Halima's brother, her replacement, in the kitchen were standing.

'No water', I said to Hamed.' The lady in the off license says we can use hers. What can we use to fetch the water?'

Looking around I only had a couple of buckets which I used to bleach the floor tiles.

'Use these', said Hamed pointing to two empty 5 gallon plastic containers from Macro that we used for the oil in the kitchen.

I marched across the street to the off license with the two drums and the lady owner showed me into a back room where there was a sink.

Quickly filling the two drums I dragged them back to the Dom Miguel and Hamed immediately emptied them into half a dozen huge pans ready to start cooking the vegetables.

'Need another twenty of these to fill the dish washer', said Hamed.

He was not kidding I went to and fro between the off license and restaurant at least another dozen times humping the heavy containers until the dishwasher was full enough to switch on. I was absolutely knackered by now and my trousers were dripping with water from the splashbacks from the taps when filling the damn things.

Next the glasswasher and coffee machine which consumed another three or four loads of the water.

'What about the toilets?' said Hamed. 'You need water, you can't send customers down the road to go to the loo'.

'I can use these buckets', I replied. 'I'll stick a notice on the loos to tell customers to flush the toilets with the water in the buckets...no problem'.

As each customer arrived that evening I explained the challenge as they were about to sit down explaining the procedure they would have to follow if they got caught short.

During the evening my main job was to quickly rush into the toilet which a customer had just used to check that firstly they had remembered to use the bucket of water to flush the loo and then once they had to refill the bucket from the container ready for the next customer.

The whole night continued in this fashion either refilling the buckets, flushing the loo's or refilling the containers from the off licence depending upon the most urgent need. Not the best job in the world and just as I was leaving for the night the water suddenly returned.

The water theme continued during the following afternoon. Directly opposite the Dom Miguel was an Indian restaurant and I began to notice some odd things happening such as two of the guys had begun sleeping there overnight. Also directly above the door of their restaurant was a large electrical panel which now had a series of exposed wires and cables running up the wall across the top of the roof.

This particular afternoon Mahed, the guy who owned the restaurant appeared in the street with a large hosepipe.

'Can I have some water, please? My water is off', he said.

'Yes, sure', I replied and he dragged the extra long hosepipe through my restaurant into the kitchen and switched on the tap.

After about one hour I was becoming a little concerned as my first customers would be arriving soon.

I wandered back across the street.

'You will have to stop now', I said. 'Customers are due, and Hamed needs to use the tap in the kitchen'.

'Ok', replied Mahed, and he instructed one of his many minions to pull back the hosepipe.

The next morning as I pulled up to unload my car the place was swarming with police. I quickly jumped back into the car to move it from it's illegal parking slot and headed for the port to park in the official car park about 400 metres away.

Returning to the restaurant to pick up my trolley ready to unload the car the police were trying to smash open the doors to the Indian restaurant with a large metal battering ram.

Once inside they quickly rounded up about six Indian chaps and handcuffed them, four of whom I had never seen before moving them into their awaiting police transit vans.

A locksmith next appeared and began to change the locks while a guy in a suit began to stick official looking posters along the windows and doors of the restaurant.

This obviously by now had drawn a large crowd eager to be part of the excitement including Barry and Karen.

Karen who was Spanish speaking read the notice.

The restaurant had been operating illegally for the last 6 months. Apparently they had been served notice by the landlord to vacate the premises. The Indian chaps not only had not paid any rent during that time had also had their electric cut off by the landlord and had been using electric from a premises in the next street. Hence the cables running over the roof.

From my point of view I was sorry to see them leave as they were always good for a bottle of gas or two and also for providing many, many food items that I always managed to either forget or run out of in the Dom Miguel.

On the day after on returning to the restaurant with the car after a large shop I parked as usual outside the cafe bar in my illegal spot ready for my quick sprint for the trolley. Having just reached the door of the restaurant big Ron came charging towards me.

'Move the bloody car', he shouted.

'Shit', I replied, assuming that the local police had arrived, and dashed back to the car.

I could hear police sirens heading my way and had just got into the driver's seat ready to pull away when three police cars pulled up behind and alongside me.

'That's a bit over the top'. I thought to myself expecting the usual bollocking and pending fines.

Ron appeared at the passenger door.

'The Celtic Bar has been broken into', he said. The Celtic Bar was next door to the cafe.

'Get going', he shouted.

I slowly reversed back onto the main road making sure I did not collide with the police cars and headed off up the road without a word from the now eight or nine police who were now wandering towards the Celtic bar. Lucky escape I thought to myself.

Towards the end of February Halima's brother decided to leave the kitchen much to the relief of Hamed who spent most of the night shouting at him which meant I had to advertise for a new kitchen assistant.

I had no sooner posted the advert on the restaurant door when I was approached by an English chap, about six foot two inches tall and weighing in at around eighteen stones called Sam asking about the job.

Apparently he was a very qualified chef but was willing to act as sous chef to provide himself with an income.

Sam started the following night and immediately was given his instructions from Hamed who quickly set the boundaries of responsibility. I could hear Hamed in the kitchen.

'Right, you prepare the starters, let me show you each one', said Hamed.

'Next you wash all of the dishes and cutlery', he continued and began to show him a couple of times how the dishwasher worked.

'At end of the evening, you mop and bleach the floor and clean the walls and benches...OK'.

Sam set to work the first night and even though it was February the kitchen must have been hovering around the forty degree mark. I noticed after about two hours that his hair was sodden and rivers of sweat were running down his face and dripping off the end of his nose, probably onto the food he was busy preparing.

When we were a little quiet he walked outside for a quick smoke, his clothes absolutely soaked in sweat and collapsed on the pavement looking as if he had just finished 10 rounds with Mike Tyson.

I walked outside, 'Are you OK?' I asked.

'Yes, fine', he replied. 'It's just been a while since I worked in a kitchen'.

At the end of the evening I asked Hamed if Sam had been OK.

'Too fat and too slow', he said, as he handed me my meal for the evening.

Sam lasted two days.

I then employed a Polish girl as assistant for Hamed, who broke Sam's record but only lasted five days in total.

Hamed was not impressed. 'North Europeans don't know hard work', he said, 'All very soft like babies'.

The following week while I was still advertising for a replacement Hamed came into the restaurant with a young Moroccan lady called Hajar who was the spitting image of Halima telling me that she would be working in the kitchen from now on.

I didn't argue and he was proved to be right as usual.

A continual problem running any restaurant were the dreaded cockroaches which always tended to exhibit themselves when we had customers in the restaurant. We were always on guard and luckily had a service contract with a pest control company when their numbers started to increase who normally sorted out the problem for a couple of months quite efficiently.

Things escalated to another level one day when I arrived at the restaurant after my daily shop to see a mouse perched on a wooden ledge just below the coffee machine. The mouse just looked at me raised up on its two hind legs as if to say, 'Who the hell are you?' I moved towards the mouse and stopped about two yards away as it just sat there laughing at me. I picked up a large baguette which was the closest thing to hand and lunged towards the mouse. At the last second it darted behind the fridge under the coffee machine and disappeared.

Thinking that this was a one off event I put this mini crisis to the back of my mind until the next morning when I arrived at the usual time. He was there again in exactly the same place standing on his two hind legs looking across at me.

'You've got to go, sorry Mickey', I said and the mouse continued to look across at me without moving. I am sure it understood what I was saying. This time I just continued to put all of the food into the cupboards and fridges talking to the mouse still sat across the other side of the bar.

After a minute or so the mouse appeared to be bored with my conversation and again shot down behind the fridge looking for better stimulation than what I could provide.

I rang the pest control guys that morning who arrived promptly with their potent anti rodent food which they pushed under the fridge and left. That evening when I returned to open the restaurant I moved the fridge forward to find Mickey lying quite still and stiff against the wall.

'Sorry mate', I said picking him up with a paper towel and sticking him in the bin feeling quite sad and guilty at the loss. I think I need a break.

At the end of February Catherine my waitress told me that she had been offered a job running a karaoke bar and would be leaving the following week.

Business was now picking up again and with the terrace now beginning to be used a little as the nights warmed up I needed to recruit two new service staff.

In the restaurant that night I was chatting to a couple of customers about the business in general and mentioned that I was looking for two new staff from next week.

The couple lived in France where they had a small business running a number of gites on behalf of someone else and because it was still winter in France they didn't have much to do at the moment. The chap called Ray was ex army, about six foot four, in his late thirties with a bald head and blonde ponytail running down his back. He was a very confident sounding chap and had certainly lived a full life. His wife Alison stood at around four foot tall, and together they really did look like the original odd couple.

They offered to come across to Spain and work in the restaurant for me. I said Ok and didn't really expect to hear from them.

Ray kept in touch by sms over the next few days and on the third day he sent a message saying that they had sorted out somewhere to stay and they were arriving on the Friday ready to start work. He also sent me his new address in Mijas, a small village about two miles inland and asked me to drop in for lunch on the Saturday.

Ray came into work for the first time on the following Monday dressed in what looked like a tuxedo with a black dickey bow and red waist coat looking like he was about to go for his regimental dinner.

He was a real asset in the restaurant, especially confident at talking to customers and organising sing songs and Happy Birthdays etc for customers who had something to celebrate.

His wife Alison would always come down to the restaurant at closing time to meet him for a quick drink and sometimes used to help with the washing up or general tidying up until he was ready to leave.

At the time the two of us were running the service but starting to struggle a little on the busy nights so I offered Alison a job mainly behind the bar serving drinks and washing glasses which proved to be a big mistake from my point of view.

During the next three or four weeks I had had to speak to Alison on more than one occasion about basically how to pull a pint of lager. There was a knack in making sure that the draught pint of lager, which needed to be served with fizz bubbling in the glass and a reasonable head on the top. There was a certain way of doing this when filling the glass. What she was serving resembled a beer that had been left out overnight, completely flat.

Also, I was becoming aware with a problem with Ray. During quiet times he stood at the door looking for customers but due to his size, dress and ponytail seemed to be putting customers off when they saw such an imposing figure standing there. His ability to pull in customers was close to zero and I eventually broke it to him that I felt that he was putting off the new customers and asked him to stay inside the restaurant while I did the PR role by the door which did not go down very well.

My problems with his wife Alison and Ray created a strained atmosphere between the three of us and I began to regret employing them both.

During mid April after about six weeks when my wife Barbara was in Fuengirola for a four day visit things came to a head one night when Hamed had taken all of the kitchen towels from the bar which he used in the kitchen for handling the hot food.

Alison who now always looked miserable piped up.

'I told you to get some new towels. Where are they?' she demanded, 'I cannot dry the glasses with dirty towels'.

I couldn't remember her asking me for any new towels and replied 'Sorry, will get some tomorrow, you will just have to use those tonight'.

'I'm not bloody using these', she said quite angrily.

I basically ignored her comments and as I often did at the end of the night went to the coffee machine for a quick espresso'.

As usual I put the ground coffee into the ladle before tightening the handle on the coffee machine outlet to make a coffee.

As I waited for the fresh coffee to pour into the cup a splurge of black gunk appeared in my cup rather than the usual smooth black liquid.

I immediately looked at the ladle and found that the metal filter was missing from inside the small ladle which was used to capture the coffee grounds.

Checking a second ladle close by I also noticed that the filter there was also missing.

'Where are the filters?' I said to Alison.

'What filters?' she replied with her usual miserable expression.

'The metal filters that sit inside the small cups to catch the coffee dregs', I said.

'No idea', she replied.

I looked in the garbage bin behind the bar which was full of empty bottles and paper towels and tablecloths from the evening's business and began to dig down towards the bottom of the bin with my fingers.

Right at the bottom I found the two metal filters and put them by the sink under the bar to wash.

'Oh', said Alison, 'They must have come out when I was banging them against the bin to empty out the old coffee'.

'Can you be more careful?' I replied, 'I have no idea where I would be able to get replacements for these'.

Alison wandered across to speak to Ray and came across to the bar where I was cashing up.

'Can we have our pay for the last three days?' said Ray.

'Sure, no problem', I replied and began to add up the hours worked between them and count out the cash from the till'.

I handed them the money.

''Right that's it, we're off', said Ray as they both turned around to walk towards the door.

The next morning as Barbara and I were having our breakfast in the local cafe I text Ray to ask if they would be in that evening still not quite sure what he had meant the night before.

'No thanks', was the reply.

I said to Barbara, 'Great news, they will not be coming back', as I finished my coffee completely unconcerned and slightly relieved.

The Sale

I had now lost count of the number of service staff I had employed in the last 11 months or so but the next recruits proved to be the best by far and stayed with me to the end.

Firstly, I recruited a young English girl called Jan who was an incredibly hard worker and could have run the place without me being there.

Secondly, I recruited Jason who was Jim's son. Jim is the guy mentioned at the start of this book who gave me a lift back to Fuengirola when the transporter came to pick up my car on the road to Ronda.

I knew Jason quite well as he was often part of the regular group, together with Barry, Ron and Dave who went out on a Friday night to play pool tournaments.

Jason was a builder by trade and I had used him occasionally to do odd jobs in the restaurant such as fix electrics or tiles in the kitchen. Jason also happened to earn money by being a David Beckham lookalike and often went to events up and down the coast to make a bit of extra cash.

Normally Jason looked like your typical scruffy builder but he could transform himself with the right clothes, hairstyle and pseudo diamond earring into an extremely good likeness to the man himself.

One evening after such an event still dressed up I saw him in one of the nearby squares with two other look alikes, Ronaldo the goofy centre forward from Brazil and Ronaldinho the other goofy footballer from Barcelona with the long greasy hair.

The square was awash with tourists taking photographs of the three of them especially the young girls and they were lapping it up.

Jason although not the most reliable of staff was unbelievable at pulling in customers to the restaurant young or old.

Whenever a group of young girls appeared by the menu outside Jason would be out there in a flash using his charm to pull them inside.

Once inside, Jason would more often than not spend time sitting with the girls at their table chatting with them rather than working, but for me this was really not a problem as he was incredibly good for the business.

It was the older women who paid the most attention to Jason often dragging their husbands back to the restaurant a second time during their holiday to have photographs taken with him.

He did however have a Spanish girlfriend who often came to the restaurant just to keep an eye on him.

Business during April and May was well ahead of the previous year and we were establishing a really good reputation down the strip.

At the end of March the lease on my apartment lapsed and due to the fact that I was looking to sell up I did not renew it despite an offer from the landlord to reduce my monthly rent from 900 to 600 euros plus service charges.

I guess that landlord was not used to being paid on time and he looked quite sad the day he came to see me to return my month's deposit.

Instead I had heard of a 'hostel' within easy walking distance of the restaurant charging 100 euros a week which included all heating and electric costs.

Jim, Jason's dad, helped me move into my new accommodation in the first week in April. It basically was one large room with two single beds, one dressing table, a large cupboard running almost the length of one wall and a small shower stuck in the corner. The loo was outside in the corridor just outside of my front door.

Jim and I with two cars moved all of my belongings out of the apartment squeezing some into one of the cupboards in the restaurant and the rest jam packed into the cupboard of my new room.

I actually loved it, it was perfect for me.

For the first time I had full English TV, a kettle, laptop and iron with ironing board in the corner of the room but best of all the room was cleaned every day and the sheets changed regularly which never really happened at the apartment unless Barbara was in town.

The only problem I found was that I did not have a washing machine to wash the linen tablecloths which I needed to do every day.

The answer was there staring me in the face...a plastic bucket.

Every night before bed I would fill the bucket with hot water and hand wash all of the tablecloths and sometimes the odd shirt or two in the bucket. Then I would hang them up across the shower in the corner to dry. The only problem was the drip, drip, drip from the washing which went on for most of the night similar to a Japanese water torture, but like anything else you get used to it. The next morning I would take the tablecloths out of the shower which had stopped dripping by now and hang them on a plastic clothes drier in my room with the window left open to dry them off while I was out doing my daily chores. Perfect, all ready to iron before the next shift at the restaurant. I often wondered what the cleaner made of it.

Barbara came to visit again for a few days at the end of May and was flabbergasted at my new living arrangements comparing my fantastic room to some sort of hovel. She actually refused to stay there especially with the dripping clothes and tablecloths and booked herself into a local hotel.

The first night she booked the hotel room I stayed with her for one night only. I found that I couldn't actually operate being separated from my daily routine especially the washing and had to return back to my room to be sure that my routine was not compromised. Still every second of every day was scheduled like clockwork from 7am in the morning until 1am the following night and nothing could be allowed to interfere with that routine.

Eventually Barbara grudgingly moved into the room with me for the last two days of her visit.

By June the restaurant was buzzing and I was managing with the help of Jason in particular to make good profits.

There was some apparent interest in buying the restaurant from an English chap called Gordon who explained that his son was looking to buy somewhere in Spain and that he had recently had a lottery win.

Gordon came to the restaurant one evening with his son in tow who was in his late teens but looked about twelve years old and we started chatting.

'Do you want to see the books?' I asked Gordon, as I did have my own unofficial books showing the incomings and outgoings on a daily basis which with some slight tweaks looked very healthy.

'Next week', replied Gordon. 'We are coming back. Let's do it then?'

'Fine', I replied.

Gordon did come back the following week on his own and made an excuse that his son was moving house and couldn't make it so we would have to all meet again later in the week.

Later that week as usual Gordon arrived again without his son making another excuse for the delay and I was beginning to doubt that he really was interested in buying.

This went on for a few more days with Gordon always promising that his son would be here tomorrow. After a while I was beginning to think that he was doing this just to make himself look important rather than anything else so began to ignore his promises altogether. Some people are really weird.

I now had a good set of regulars returning to the restaurant particularly friends such as Dave and Sonia, big Ron and Molly and Barry and Karen.

One particular night Dave and Sonia were in having a meal. On the table beside theirs were seven British girls who Jason had obviously managed to drag in who were celebrating a hen party.

The girls were naturally quite merry and loud and were drinking quite heavily a combination of wine and vodka. At the end of their meal they were waving at me trying to get my attention to give them the bill without success.

Dave saw this and came across the bar offering to take the bill across to them for me.

I totted up the bill and handed Dave a slip for 320 euros to take across to them and he brought back the cash plus tips for their meals to the till.

After the girls left Dave came across to the bar.

'320 euros', he said. 'I don't make that in a week'.

Dave owned a small cafe bar off one of the side streets running off Fish Alley with three tables outside and four inside the cafe mainly serving drinks and a few light snacks. He sat in his cafe from morning until late at night normally looking bored out of his mind.

Dave was aware I was looking to sell the Dom Miguel.

'How much do you want for this place?' said Dave.

'166,000 euros', I replied.

'Leave it with me', said Dave. 'I want to buy this place but I need to sell my bar first.'

'Ok, I replied', 'But if I can sell it sooner I will be out of here'.

For the next couple of nights Dave often came back to the Dom Miguel to help and find out how the restaurant was being run. I really wanted Dave to have it.

One night in June as I was working manically on the terrace with Jason dragging in customers a couple of Italian chaps who were tucking into a paella called me across.

They introduced themselves as Alonzo and Enzio who were brothers from Naples. Alonzo who was the elder of the two brothers was a big guy around six foot tall and seventeen stones. His brother

Enzio was a shorter chap wearing glasses who looked like an accountant.

'Is this place for sale?' asked Alonzo who wasn't aware that I had it for sale with the local agents.

'Everything's for sale', I replied. 'Make me an offer?'

'What do you want?' said Alonzo.

'166,000 euros', I replied after pretending to think for a while.

Alonzo nodded and went back to finishing his meal.

Before he left he told me he would be back in two weeks with his mother so that she could see the place for herself.

As usual in my typical sceptical fashion I thought that would be the end of it.

At the end of June as again I was using my well practised lines to draw customers into the restaurant I started a conversation with an elderly lady with her six year old granddaughter in tow. She was looking for pizza.

I managed to talk them through the door when after around five minutes two guys came through the door and sat down at their table. It was Alonzo and Enzio, and this was their mother and Alonzo's daughter, Maria.

'Are you still interested?' I asked Alonzo.

'Yes', he replied. 'Can we talk?'

'Can you come back tomorrow?' I asked. 'I don't want my chef to know I might be selling the place. It is actually up for sale with Fiesta

Properties. Their office is beside the Los Palmeras hotel down the road. Probably best if you tell them that you are interested'.

'Ok', replied Alonzo.

'We will go and see them and come back at 2pm tomorrow. You can show us around then.'

The next morning I received an early call from Stuart the Fiesta Properties boss saying that they would all be arriving at the restaurant at 2pm.

At 2pm the five of them arrived at the restaurant for a proper viewing. I had made sure that the place was spotless during the morning ready for the visit and they were very impressed.

I also showed them the accounts which I kept, like I say with a few minor tweaks covering the nights when takings were poor.

'What do you think?' said Stuart, obviously keen on the sale.

'Looks fantastic', said Alonzo looking at his mother who was obviously footing the bill.

'Ok if you want it, let's do it', said the mother and we all shook hands.

'I will work with you for a few days when you take over, there's quite a bit to learn', I said.' Also will you keep the staff?'

'Great', they replied, 'And yes we will keep all of the staff'.

Stuart then took us all through the sales process for which I was now familiar, especially the need to transact totally in cash.

The family were returning to Italy the next day and we arranged to meet at the office of Fiesta Properties on Wednesday 16th July to complete the deal with their abogado.

I immediately rang Barbara who was very pleased with the news and she arranged to fly to Fuengirola on the Tuesday. I also contacted Alberto the landlord who was obviously very pleased to pick up another wad of cash for doing bugger all. This time the sale price to him was 110,000 euros or as far as he was concerned 22,000 euros in his back pocket. I wonder if he ever submitted capital gains tax returns...maybe I know the answer.

Barbara arrived on the 15th and after finishing what we thought would be our last shift in the restaurant we were ready.

At the end of the night we sat down with Hamed and the rest of the staff to tell them our plans and to reassure them that their jobs were safe.

The next day we arrived at Stuart's office as planned. It was buzzing. Inside the office Alonzo and Enzio were sat with their abogado discussing what was about to happen during the exchange.

Myself, Barbara, Carlos my gestor who insisted he should be there, together with Alberto the landlord and Alberto's partner waited outside on the pavement waiting to be called in to the office.

We waited and waited for around one hour on the pavement all becoming more and more anxious, especially Carlos.

'I'll go inside and see what they are doing?' said Carlos.

Carlos returned shaking his head after a few minutes.

He spoke to Alberto the landlord first in Spanish and we looked across as Alberto began walking down the road away from the office.

'There is a problem', said Carlos,' They do not have the money'.

'So what do we do?' I asked.

'There is nothing we can do', said Carlos.

Stuart appeared at the door looking shell shocked and Alonzo with his brother walked past us and off down the road without a word.

'Bollocks', I said to Barbara as stunned we both set off back to the restaurant thinking what to say to Hamed and the rest of them. I had not done any of my normal shopping duties that day so set off to stock up ready to open again that evening.

That evening Hamed as usual arrived first.

'Where are the new people?' he said.

'They did not have any money', I replied, 'We are not selling'.

The next morning myself and Barbara still disappointed were walking along the promenade looking for somewhere to have lunch and I spotted Alonzo sat alone in a cafe.

'Should I go and talk to him?' I said to Barbara.

'Not sure', she replied.

'Ah, what is there to lose', I thought and I went across to sit at his table.

Alonzo looked surprised to see us standing there.

'What happened?' I said. 'Do you not want the restaurant now?'

'Yes, I still want to buy it. It's my brother he now doesn't want to come to Spain', said Alonzo.

'So where does that leave us', I replied.

'I need to speak to my mother in Italy and Enzio again', he said.

'OK', I replied, 'But you've seen the books, things will be very busy the next few months and I will not be selling in September, October', and left him on his own at the table convinced that that would be the last time I would set eyes on him.

Life continued as normal in the Dom Miguel and Barbara had now gone back to the UK when Stuart from Fiesta Properties walked into the restaurant out of the blue the following week.

'It's back on', he said. Alonzo and his mother are flying in on Tuesday next week to buy the restaurant'.

'What about the brother?' I asked.

'He's staying in Italy. Alonzo's wife is now coming over to work with him straight away'.

'Great', I said, 'What time do you want me?'

'2pm at the office, Tuesday afternoon', said Stuart.

'No, can we make it 10 in the morning. If he decides to mess me around again I need time to do the shopping ready to open. I don't trust him', I said.

'OK, let's make it 10am on the Wednesday morning then', replied Stuart, 'I'll let them know'.

'Will your wife be here?' said Stuart.

'No, doesn't need to be. I have Power of Attorney set up so I can sign on her behalf', I replied.

'Give me the Power of Attorney papers now and I'll make sure Alonzo's solicitor is OK with them. We don't want any more excuses'.

I handed over the papers signed by the Notary's office and Stuart left the restaurant.

Still very sceptical about the outcome of next week I just continued as normal in the restaurant not telling a soul of the plans, not even Carlos.

On the Wednesday I set off for the estate agents office still not convinced that it would all go smoothly.

On arriving at the office I was met by Stuart who introduced me to Alonzo's abogado Lionel. Alonzo's mother, wife and daughter were sitting by the window. Alberto the landlord was standing outside on the pavement.

'Are we ready?' said Lionel the abogado.

'First Philip can you check the cash is what it should be', he said.

Stuart suggested I went into another room to check and I went into the room alone to check the money which should be 144,000 euros in cash.

I counted the money carefully...100,000 euros. I counted it again to make sure and it definitely was 44,000 euros light.

From the door I called Stuart into the room.

'Stuart, can you re check this. I make it 100,000 euros', I said.

Stuart sat down and again carefully counted what was on the table.

'Yes, that's 100,000 euros', he confirmed.

We both walked back into the other room where the rest of the group were sitting.

'There's only 100,000 euros here', I said. There should be an extra 44,000'.

Panic set in among Alonzo and his family as they carefully checked their bags.

'Here it is', said Alonzo. 'It was in this other packet... sorry'.

I took the packet from him and went back into the office with Stuart to check.

'Yes, that's correct', I said to Stuart, 'Can you double check'.

Stuart rechecked the cash and confirmed that it was all there.

We both walked back into the office and sat down. There was a sense of relief and a little embarrassment from Alonzo.

We all signed the new contract as directed by Lionel and we all shook hands.

Finally Alberto was ushered into the room to pick up his 22,000 euros which he quickly checked and immediately left the office.

'Do you want to come in tonight and I will show you the ropes', I said to Alonzo and his family.

'And tomorrow I will take you shopping'.

'You can start for real, tomorrow night if you want. I will work with you for a few days. By the way here are the details of the credit card machine. You need to change it to your account straight away'.

We all shook hands again and left the office. It was all done.

I walked down the road back to the hostel very aware that I was carrying 144,000 euros in a plastic bag. 'Got to get to the bank in the morning', I said to myself feeling very conspicuous.

I immediately text Barbara back in the UK with the message... 'All done now. Arrange for the car to be shipped back'.

My phone rang within seconds as I reconfirmed the good news to Barbara.

That evening I broke the news to the staff who did not seem to be surprised.

At around 7.30pm Alonzo and his family all arrived at the restaurant and I quickly introduced them to the staff. Hamed could also speak fluent Italian which was obviously a bonus.

They all sat down for a meal and I made an extra effort to pull customers in that night to make the place look extra busy. I wondered to myself how to explain my Big Willey's chat up line to a bunch of Italians.

I asked Alonzo if he wanted me to show him how the till worked but he declined saying that he had had enough stress for one day and would start tomorrow for real.

I arranged to meet them at 10am the next day on the dot for the Malaga run giving me time to put half of the cash into my Spanish bank account to transfer back to my UK account. Even at this stage my scepticism had got the better of me and I didn't trust the bank sufficiently to do the full transfer of all of the cash without any problems. Just in case I kept back 70,000 euros in cash to take with me on the plane back home.

I was at the bank at 9am ready for it to open and created quite a queue behind me as they counted out the 74,000 euros in 50 euro notes. I asked them to transfer all of the money in the Spanish bank account to my account in the UK and to close the account for good to make sure no further direct debits would be processed.

'When will it arrive in my account?' I asked the teller.

'Two to three days' she replied. I left the bank to find my car parked on the front with a parking fine stuck on the windscreen.

'They can whistle for that', I said to myself as I stuffed the parking ticket into the nearest dustbin and set off for the restaurant to pick up Alonzo.

Waiting by the restaurant I met Alonzo, his mother and six year old daughter ready for the shopping trip of their lifetime.

His wife Ora who was Cuban remained at the restaurant as the four of us set off for Malaga.

As we travelled along I was trying to explain to Alonzo all of the roads and buildings to look out for to make sure he would be able to do the journey himself in the future.

First stop Macro. I was now completely radicalised into rushing around the entire store in less than twenty minutes as I had been doing for the past year like a maniac.

With an oldish lady and six year old running behind the trolley struggling to keep up with me even though I had dropped my usual pace by around sixty percent we eventually finished the shop.

'510 euros', I said to Alonzo at the till which he duly handed over to the cashier and we returned to the car ready to drive back to Fuengirola and the next stop Lidl.

Just as we were entering the final roundabout into Fuengirola a retching and gurgling noise could be heard behind us. It was Alonzo's little daughter Maria who had thrown up in the back of the car covering her grandma in sick and also managing to cover most of herself as well.

I stopped the car and pulled up at the side of the road.

'Take us back', said the grandmother, 'Please'.

'To the restaurant?' I asked.

'Yes, take us there', she replied.

I slowly drove back to the restaurant where Ora was waiting and dropped off Maria and her grandmother.

'We'll clean the car when you both get back', she said as myself and Alonzo drove off to Lidl to continue the shopping.

In hindsight I should have taken the food from Macro out of the boot but instead we continued the dash to Lidl.

After another rush around Lidl we returned to the car to offload.

Now normally the Lidl shop would sit on the back seat of the car but it was covered in sick.

I went back to the Lidl entrance and picked up two cardboard boxes which I flattened and covered the back seat of the car, before sticking the tins, cartons and fresh vegetables on top.

We set off again to complete the shop at Mercadona. I could by now have done this in my sleep.

'Do you think you can do this yourself?' I asked Alonzo

Looking at me in partial amazement, he replied, 'No way'. At this point I think a glimmer of realisation was beginning to dawn on him as to what he was letting himself in for. I certainly remember the feeling after my first trip with Hue, the Chinese guy a few months before.

'Don't worry', I said, 'I am here for a few more days until you are fully trained'.

We returned to the restaurant to unload the food where Ora was waiting with a bucket of disinfectant ready to clean the car. Her daughter Maria was now full of life again and dashing around the place with her grandmother running behind her.

That night in the restaurant with Alonzo behind the bar with his wife I handed over the keys and started his training just as I had had done some sixteen months before.

The bill for the first order arrived at the till and for the first time Alonzo had to process it. I found out that his previous job had been as a CAD designer in Naples. I thought to myself that I.T. had a lot to answer for as it has been my previous life for 30 years as well.

Transfixed and with full concentration he started to enter the items from the paper bill into the till and with an expression of total satisfaction he managed to produce his first ticket ready to go back to his first customer.

'Perfect', I said. The night went well and even though we did use the credit card machine a couple of times I made sure I gave the takings back to Alonzo in cash to put in the till.

That night and the next two days and nights went extremely well and we had done around fifty or so covers each night which was pretty good going.

On the third night it was not so good. Despite my best efforts I struggled to reach the quarter full target and takings went right down to around the 350 euro figure. I could see the look of disappointment on Alonzo's face and tried to explain that one poor night would always happen now and again during the summer. I also reassured him that September, October and early November were the most profitable months to look forward to. I knew that what I was saying was true but I did not mention the fact that you really had to work hard to pull the customers into the restaurant. However, in my defence he could see the effort I was putting in talking to customers from the doors across the terrace and making sure we had a couple of friendly tables near the menus putting in a good word to potential customers in return for a couple of free drinks.

During next two days we continued our daily trips to the shops and Alonzo was starting to become more confident although he was painfully slow.

'You must have a car', I kept repeating to him. 'I will be going back in two days'.

'My brother is driving mine from Naples. It should be here by the end of the week', replied Alonzo.

Like myself during my first few months Alonzo stayed in safety behind the bar away from the customers managing the till and the drinks orders while Jason and Jan ran the service with the real customers. I knew that he was not comfortable talking to customers out front, but that was not my problem now.

Boxto the Final Story

On the third day I checked my bank account and the money had been transferred successfully back to my U.K account. It was also the day that my car was being shipped back to the U.K.

This takes us right back to the beginning of the book where I had arranged to meet the transporter on the road to Ronda with Jim. I had crammed the car with all of my possessions, television, laptop, music centre, power drill, karcher pressure washer and filling every other available space with clothes and a few bottles of spirits.

Things felt very strange for me after I dropped off the car for the first time not being crazily busy for 18 hours a day and it was really surreal. I really didn't know how to fill in my newly found free time and spent most of my remaining days completely lost and aimlessly wandering between the 'Pig' and Dave and Karen and Barry's cafes. I was even helping Dave to serve in his bar for something to do some of the time.

One more major thing before I left Fuengirola was to talk to Roberto about Boxto and what his plans were.

On my final full day in Fuengirola I arranged a meeting with Roberto for 2pm in a cafe on the front. During that morning I was just lazily passing my time as usual sitting in Dave's bar chatting.

Completely out of the blue a Spanish chap approached me who I did not recognise at first. It was Juan the landlord of Boxto, the guy I used to give the 1,000 euro rent to every month until Roberto took over.

He was asking me about Roberto explaining that he had been trying to get hold of him.

'Well, I'm meeting him at 2 this afternoon. Come along if you want'.

'Ok, great see you there', replied Juan who then went on his way.

At 2pm I arrived to find Roberto sat drinking a coffee with Juan at the bar seemingly ordering a drink for himself. It looked a little odd to me as normally you would just sit waiting to be served. The two were obviously not best of friends at the moment.

I shook hands with Roberto and Juan and the three of us sat down.

Juan started the conversation looking at me.

'Has he', looking at Roberto 'Given you any money since he took over Boxto'.

'No, not a cent', I replied.

'Thought so', said Juan who then turned to Roberto.

'Where is my rent?'

'I've paid you', said Roberto indignantly.

'The last rent you paid was May where is June and the July payment is due next week. I have a little baby and cannot afford food or rent and my wife is sick', said Juan.

I was just sat listening thinking well why don't you get a bloody job, when Roberto's Spanish mannerisms started to kick in.

'I was robbed, my flat was robbed. They took 2,000 euros', said Roberto.

'So you have been running Boxto now for about ten months and you are telling me that all you have made is 2,000 euros, I said, 'You told me you knew what you were doing. I bet you made more than that on New Year's Eve alone'.

Roberto then moved into the usual tosh I had heard many, many times.

'Spanish have no money, no people come'…….on and on it went.

'You give me 2,000 euros and I promise I can make it all better for you', now moving into the praying and pained expression position.

'No chance', I replied. 'Would you trust this guy?' I said to Juan turning towards him.

'Come with me, come with me now. I will show you', said Roberto

We both followed him to his apartment which was on the first floor above a small shop.

We walked in and there was a window on the far wall.

'They used a ladder and climbed in there', said Roberto pointing to the window.

'Is that what you have brought us here. To show us your bloody window'.

'Yes now you believe me', said Roberto with a pained expression now fixed across his face.

'Not really', I replied.

'Look', I said. 'I am going back to the UK tomorrow, now the restaurant is sold'.

'I need to speak to my abogado before making any decision. I will be back next week and I will arrange a meeting for the three of us with him for next Thursday at 10am in his office'.

'I will be there', said Juan.

'What about you?' I said to Roberto.

'Yes, yes, I will come', he replied.

Before I left Fuengirola to head home I briefly managed to speak to Carlos and explained the situation with regards to Boxto. Carlos said he would pass the information on to Antonio and confirmed the meeting time for 10am on the following Thursday morning.

I said my goodbyes to Dave, big Ron and Barry and Karen and headed off to the airport to fly back to the UK.

It was around the 26th July when I landed at Manchester on what I believe was one of the hottest days ever in the UK. I thought it must be a good sign.

The following Wednesday I headed back to Fuengirola for the planned meeting the next day.

Walking into the office Carlos shouted across the room.

'Come and see me before you leave. There are a few things to sign before you go'.

I nodded towards Carlos and was ushered into a small room where Roberto and Juan were sitting still not really speaking to each other.

Antonio entered the room.

'Phil, come with me. I need to speak to you alone first', he said and we walked into an adjoining larger office.

'Carlos has told me. Roberto owes two months rent, yes?' said Antonio.

'Yes that's correct', I replied.

'And if you pay it what will you do next?' said Antonio. 'You live back in England now'.

'I've no idea. What can I do?' I replied.

'Just give the bar back to Juan is what I would do and go', said Antonio.

'If Juan is happy with that he will not push to be paid his rent money', he continued.

'Yes, there is no other choice really is there', I replied

'OK', said Antonio. 'I'll ask them to come in now'.

Antonio opened the door and Roberto and Juan came into the room.

Antonio explained the decision on my behalf to Juan who happily accepted the arrangement.

'I want to take all of the drinks out of Boxto before I give it to you', I said, just looking I suppose for a crumb of comfort I could glean from this hopeless situation.

'No problem', said Juan. 'Meet me at 10am tomorrow at Boxto and you can have the drinks'.

'Anything else?' said Antonio.

'Yes, the keys', I replied turning to Roberto. 'Give me the keys'.

'I can run it for you', said Roberto.

'Give me the keys', I repeated.

Roberto handed me the keys which I passed across to Juan. I had lost Boxto.

Feeling a little down about the situation I left the office when I realised that Carlos had asked to see me before I went.

I turned round to walk back to see Carlos and was just about at the office entrance when I turned back again and started walking away from the building, thinking to myself. 'That's it, the end, finito'. I don't really want to see him. My time in Spain was over. I did feel bad about not going to see Carlos again before I left as he really had been my most trustworthy friend during my time in Fuengirola but I just needed to get away.

That evening I met with Dave and told him that he could have all of the drinks from Boxto free of charge. Like I said it was really only a final gesture I was making and not really necessary.

The following morning Dave and I turned up at Boxto as arranged to meet Juan who was busy inspecting the place when we arrived.

As we were just moving the first couple of crates out of the club Roberto appeared with two young Spanish ladies in tow.

Roberto started speaking to Juan about taking the new till which had replaced the previous one stolen a few months earlier.

'Phil, tell him it is my till, tell him to give it to me', said Roberto turning to me.

'Not my problem. In fact I am sick of listening to your bloody voice to be honest. Why don't you shut the fuck up and do us all a favour', I replied and continued to grab the crates of drink.

The discussion became quite heated and the two young ladies joined in shouting and waving their arms around.

Myself and Dave ignored the show and continued to go back into the club for more bottles and crates.

As we were about to enter the door into Boxto one of the ladies stood in the doorway stopping us from entering and shouting at me and Dave to stop what we were doing.

I pushed past her not so politely asking her who the hell she was and to not so politely bugger off out of the way.

The noise levels rose quite a bit and from across the road two local policemen joined in the fun.

In the middle of the din Juan was trying to explain to the police what was going on.

One of the policemen grabbed Roberto and escorted him to the other side of the road. The second policeman stood in front of the mad screaming women gently pushing them both backwards into the street.

One of the policemen turned to me and Dave indicating that we could carry on emptying the place of drink.

Finally, we fully loaded the two cars and drove to Dave's cafe to stash the drinks. Quite a good deal for Dave for a free cooked breakfast that day.

Finally it was over. I flew back to the UK the next day for good..adventure over.

Final Thoughts

Looking back now at my time in Fuengirola I have no regrets about the experience but I was very lucky.

There are thousands of bars and restaurants all competing for business. Most of the established places are Spanish owned which have built their reputations over many years.

Most businesses owned by British will struggle to make any sort of money and many just walk away with nothing to show for it. You find quickly that the Spanish only use Spanish restaurants and bars. Steve was on a loser to nothing from day one.

I was very lucky to have a great chef, without whom I would not have had any business at all. Good chef's are not ten a penny on the Costa del Sol.

In addition, the success I had when I finally turned the business around was due to absolute bloody mindedness and determination to squeeze any potential profits and maximise footfall single handedly. This involved working 18 hours a day with a combination of shopping, cleaning, setting up the restaurant each day, managing staff, accounts and finally serving until the last customer left. The main priority was to do anything to pull customers inside the restaurant. There was no slack at all within this relentless schedule day after day.

The myth about sitting in the sun looking out at the sea will last for about ten days. The novelty will soon wear off and all you want to do is to sit somewhere cool and catch up on your sleep.
During my entire stay I visited the beach on two occasions and sunbathed on the balcony once for two hours. The heat especially

when you are working 16 hours a day is oppressive and all that you do is try and avoid it.

I found the challenge quite exciting although stressful for the first six months as I was continually learning new skills and making lots of changes either to reduce costs or drum up more and more business. After the first six months I found the days incredibly boring, repetitive, tedious and very, very long. My brain was in total autopilot and any change to my schedule completely knocked me for six. The nights depended mostly on how busy we were. A busy restaurant certainly improves your mood massively. An empty restaurant is the most stressful feeling in the world.

I did change completely. From being able to deal with people in a rational manner I changed into being absolutely suspicious of everyone, especially the Spanish. I trusted no-one based on my experiences with most suppliers, the police and the solicitor all trying their best to rip me off and my manner became very abrupt with the Spanish towards the end of my stay there. It actually reached the point where I did not want them to come into the restaurant at all.

I remember in the early days almost grovelling with them trying to meet their demands to ensure they enjoyed their time in the restaurant. In the end I made little effort to even try and speak Spanish when dealing with them.
When I heard them speaking Spanish by the menu I literally turned my attention elsewhere.

My advice to anyone thinking of moving abroad to run a restaurant would be.

Firstly, check the seasons for the core business. On the Costa del Sol the season runs from February to November. The season in places like the Costa Blanca or Greek Islands will run from March to October. You must check the businesses out of season, as you still have to pay the bills over the winter. Finally make sure that you have a good chef. Without a good chef you will have no business. Unless you are an experienced chef don't even consider trying to complete over 180 courses a night.

Cafe bars will not make any money and need to be open for long hours. You are talking normally less than 4 euros a cover and you need to sell a lot of coffee. The restaurant in the end was making close to 16 euros per customer and open about a third of the time compared to your standard all day cafe.

Never take over a business where your main custom is Spanish, make sure that they are mainly British. Spanish customers will soon disappear. The Spanish on the Costa Del Sol only frequent their own restaurants and bars.

There are literally hundreds of businesses up for sale on the Costa del Sol and competition is fierce. In fact I would suggest that all businesses are up for sale if you were to enquire. You need to ask yourself why. Definitely do not listen to the agents. During my time there David the agent actually introduced me to a chap from Salford who was looking to buy a bar in the grotty Fuengirola port assuming that I would speak highly of the opportunity. I told him not to do it. He did anyway. I'll give him six months.

The only people who will make money are the selling agents and to a much greater extent the landlords who as well as taking their monthly rents will churn each of their businesses regularly, probably around once a year and pull in 20% of the sale price on the new lease each time.

I have come out of the experience relatively unscathed from a financial point of view. Although I lost Boxto, the Dom Miguel just about made up the shortfall. I did check my bank accounts to tot the numbers up when I returned to the UK. Over the sixteen months I made a loss of only 2,000 euros taking all things into account.

I returned to Fuengirola in July 2007 for a visit the following year to eat at the Dom Miguel.

I sat outside on the terrace in the Dom Miguel with my wife to eat and retried my skills in pulling customers into Alonzo's restaurant. During the duration of my meal I had managed to talk in about five tables on his behalf.

Speaking to Hamed who was still there, they had had a dreadful winter. Jan and Jason were no longer working there.

'He just closed the doors and expected people to come in', said Hamed, 'Business was rubbish. He never even tried to talk to customers outside or even inside for that matter.'

'How's he managed the shopping?' I asked Hamed.

'Always forgets many things', he replied, 'Hopeless.'

While I was there I visited Boxto. To my horror it had now been renamed 'Honeys' and was being run by two young girls from East London.

I spoke to one of the girls called Julie.

'How long have you been here?' I asked.

'Six weeks', Julie replied.

'And how's business?' I enquired.

'Oh, we are just starting the summer. It's going to be fantastic', she replied.

'Good luck', I said, knowing that her chances of making money were virtually nil.

A few weeks after returning to the UK I even started looking at running a food pub local to where I lived in Cheshire.

I arranged a meeting with Punch taverns who took me through their business model, mark-ups and what the profit sharing mechanisms were.

'100% mark-up on wine and you take 50% of any profit, we get the other 50%', the guy from Punch said looking to impress me.

'My mark-up for wine in Spain was 1,000 percent, and I took 1,000 percent profit, you must be joking. You are taking the piss aren't you?'

The guy from Punch was not amused and left me very unhappy with his day's work.

My son Steve went to visit Mikey and his brother Des about nine months later to catch up with them. On the second day I received a phone call from Steve.

'Dad, I've been mugged', said Steve. This time by a bunch of Spanish youths with knives.

'Are you OK, what did they get? I replied.

'Just cash and debit card. I've cancelled the card', said Steve.

'What about your plane tickets home? I said

'They are in Des's flat', replied Steve, 'But I need some cash to get to the airport'.

'Go and see Dave', I replied. 'He will lend you a few quid to get back'.

Steve managed to borrow some cash from Dave but still managed somehow to miss the train stop for the airport ending up in downtown Malaga.

He caught the plane through pure luck a due to a one hour delay and flew back to Manchester vowing never to return.

By 2009 the Dom Miguel was up for sale in the local agents at 66,000 euros and now it was closed completely for three months of the year while Alonzo and his family returned to Italy for a long break. Dave from the Spanish Sunshine bar had lost his business deciding just to walk away from it in the end like many others before him.

I was tempted for about five seconds to buy the Dom Miguel again at the bargain price but I knew it would have killed me off due to the relentless work pattern and I would have needed Hamed my chef who by now had left the Dom Miguel to work elsewhere.

Been there done that I told myself and no doubt my wife would have killed me if I even suggested it.

However all of this did teach me one big lesson.

British people abroad have a bad reputation generally but during my time In Spain I only had the one problem and by far and away the vast majority of my customers were Brits.

They are often too polite for their own good, always apologising if they had to complain about anything and always paid the bill and gave good tips. Even the young guys although a bit rowdy at times always respected your business and never caused any real problems for me.

The same can be said of the many Irish visitors as well who were by far and away top of the wine drinking list.

Scandinavians, French and the Germans were also a good bunch to deal with generally although they did complain a bit at times and I found that the Danish and the Finish, mainly those who lived in the forest apparently, according to Adar, had no real sense of humour. I could never understand the French eating habits at all as they often wanted the three courses at the same time and eat their food in parallel ending up with a right mess all on one plate.

The Spanish outside of the Costas and Portuguese were also a decent bunch and always very polite and respectful, although their tips were notoriously bad.

Last but not least this brings me to the Spanish from the local region who I really found to be very hard work. They would sit for hours spending very little and making lots of noise often shouting across the restaurant either to me or my staff to bring them another drink or often more olive oil, much to the disdain of the other customers in the restaurant who were not impressed.

The gangs of Spanish lads who roam the streets with knives also need to be sorted out. I guess they have never known the Franco regime and just see the British especially as a bunch of badly behaved foreigners with no right to be there. They need to seriously think again before the Brits all disappear and stop going to Spain completely. There is 25% unemployment now in the 20 to 25 age group. If the Brits all up and left that figure would probably double particularly on the Costas where there are a huge number of British businesses employing the Spanish.

It is now just turned 2016, ten years since my adventure and we have all lived through the financial crisis, especially the Southern Europeans. The Spanish can now not take for granted the Brits and Germans to keep on buying property and holidaying over there to boost their economy. The recent property crash has confirmed this.

I noticed mid way through the crisis that there had been a government initiative to retrain all customer service staff in order to increase their chances of future business. I think that the penny has now dropped with them that they are still very much reliant upon their tourist economy to survive and need to up their game.

At the time there were also rules stating that non residents were subject to paying higher levels of capital gains tax than a Spanish resident when selling their properties. They are sitting on a time bomb which will no doubt bite them in the arse in the not too distant future.
The cases of property being built illegally without proper permission and being demolished also adds fuel to this fire.

Paying tax, a novelty to them at the time needs to be sorted out big time and they need to rid themselves of the petty rules, denuncias etc, which just annoy everyone. I remember one incident when I was working in Spain when someone equivalent to a parish councillor took a disliking to two of my friends who ran a steak restaurant. She demanded that they had to change all of the furniture in their restaurant because it was the wrong style and colour according to some obscure government guidelines. That was it she made the decision and it had to happen or they would have been closed down.

In my time there I paid around 150 euros in tax. Everything is done in cash to be non traceable. I wandered around every day with around 1000 euros in my back pocket for shopping, suppliers etc. I never once used a debit card nor did I need one.

I spoke to a chap in Greece a couple of years ago discussing the economy and he told me that by law you could not be thrown out of your home for non payment of the mortgage if you had nowhere else to go. He seemed very proud of the fact that anyone could buy a property with a mortgage and then just decide not to pay the mortgage back. I believe the same thing applies in Spain.

Good luck to them but one thing is for sure, I wouldn't go back there to live and work. I suggest all Brits do their homework before trying to run a restaurant in Spain. Speak to owners who are selling and ask them why. Make it obvious that you are not interested in buying from them and they may reveal the truth.

Take all business accounts shown to you with a pinch of salt and finally don't believe a word that the agents tell you.

If you are happy then to go ahead, I wish you the best of luck. You will need it.

I have tried my best to honestly relate my experiences during 2005/06 working in Spain that truly express the situation at that time. Things may have improved since, as I have read that a lot of redevelopment and a huge fight on crime has occurred in this area during the last ten years or so. I really hope so.

Finally, just like everywhere else tourists need to be careful and avoid being out on their own late at night but despite my experience as a restaurateur I would still visit the Costa resorts for my fill of sunshine, sand, sea and very good value and quality food.